The Politics of Sexual Violence

DOI: 10.1057/9781137461728.0001

Other Palgrave Pivot titles

DOI: 10.1057/9781137461728.0001

palgrave▸pivot

The Politics of Sexual Violence: Rape, Identity and Feminism

Alison Healicon
Independent Researcher, UK

palgrave
macmillan

DOI: 10.1057/9781137461728.0001

First published 2016 by
PALGRAVE MACMILLAN

Palgrave Macmillan in the UK is an imprint of Macmillan Publishers Limited, registered in England, company number 785998, of Houndmills, Basingstoke, Hampshire RG21 6XS.

Palgrave Macmillan in the US is a division of St Martin's Press LLC, 175 Fifth Avenue, New York, NY 10010.

Palgrave Macmillan is the global academic imprint of the above companies and has companies and representatives throughout the world.

Palgrave® and Macmillan® are registered trademarks in the United States, the United Kingdom, Europe and other countries.

ISBN: 978–1–137–46173–5 EPUB
ISBN: 978–1–137–46172–8 PDF
ISBN: 978–1–137–46171–1 Hardback

A catalogue record for this book is available from the British Library.

A catalog record for this book is available from the Library of Congress.

www.palgrave.com/pivot

DOI: 10.1057/9781137461728

Contents

palgrave▶**pivot**

www.palgrave.com/pivot

1
Sexual Violence

Abstract: *Chapter 1 outlines the purpose of the book which is to examine the obvious and obscure processes of compartmentalisation and categorisation that define what sexual violence is and who 'rape victims' are, with particular focus on Rape Culture in its trivialisation of rape and the psychological discourse of harm which sensationalises the 'rape victim'. To set the parameters of the book, sexual violence is defined in relation to compartmentalisation, the methodology is outlined, and participants are presented.*

Healicon, Alison. *The Politics of Sexual Violence: Rape, Identity and Feminism.* Basingstoke: Palgrave Macmillan, 2015. DOI: 10.1057/9781137461728.0002.

My experiences with the term [victim] almost universally involve revealing to someone relatively uninformed that I've been raped by someone not known to me...One memorable response was 'oh, so it was a stranger rape then?' The tone of the conversation changed completely from that moment. She wanted to know the details. Would it help me to talk about what he did, she wondered? The voyeurism was dripping from every single word. Don't get me wrong, I've had conversations where I've experienced the sigh and the 'oh, one of those' reactions when you say the man who raped you was someone close to you as well. There's usually no voyeurism there – just a strained sympathy underlined with the implication that, well, that doesn't really count then, does it? What I'd like to be better understood is that neither of these reactions is the right one. Neither is supportive. Neither is what we want women to receive when we talk about rape. We can get so caught up in our anger at the lack of acknowledgement and denial of the seriousness of rape that it almost seems like the 'shock and awe' reaction must be one to envy. It isn't. It's based on an entirely mythical conception of what the harm of rape is, and the nosiness and voyeurism surrounding something people believe to be horrific but rare. It's the cliff edge where the conversation changes from one involving you as a living, breathing person, to one about a myth in someone else's mind.

(Lyra)

Recent media interest in historic childhood sexual abuse and rape, perpetrated within institutions and by celebrities, has promoted an awareness of sexual violence and its psychological impact. However, this particular cultural framing of sexual violence is problematic because it regurgitates rape mythology and pop psychology misrepresenting sexual violence and those who have experienced rape. This book, therefore, investigates and critiques the obvious and obscure processes of compartmentalisation and categorisation, which define what sexual violence is and who 'rape victims' are, particularly within Rape Culture and the psychological discourse of harm (O'Dell 2003). Contemporary Rape Culture normalises and therefore trivialises male sexualised violence, compartmentalising and ranking 'types' of rape according to assumed severity and rarity. The psychological paradigm sensationalises the supposed symptoms

DOI: 10.1057/9781137461728.0002

of the traumatised 'rape victim'. In a process of categorisation, through pathologisation and diagnostic criteria that provide the psy-professional with tools to assess her credibility and ascertain her complicity, she is (re)produced as disreputable and diminished. Both Rape Culture and the psychological paradigm rely on a fixed and inevitably gendered essentialism that denies female agency and blames women for their own victimisation. The individualism of victim-blaming also absents from critical analysis those who are really responsible for orchestrating, perpetrating, ignoring, and excusing sexual violence.

The processes of compartmentalisation and of categorisation are problematic, as Lyra suggests, because both preclude the possibility of continuing as a 'living, breathing person'. In rape, Winkler (2002) asserts the 'victim's' sense of self is destroyed so she no longer recognises the person she was and is. In the aftermath of rape, this dehumanisation is reproduced in secondary encounters with others' expectations and judgements (Brison 2002). Standing on a metaphorical 'cliff edge' the individual is either recognised as legitimate, a 'proper victim', and invited into the 'rape victim' identity position, or rendered unbelievable and excluded from categorisation (Butler 2004). The type of sexual violence she experienced contributes to her assessment as credible. Whether recognised or not, she is defined in relation to myths and presumptions. In order to advance an alternative account that might sustain her as a 'living, breathing person', this research is grounded within the concerns of 12 women who have experienced rape either as a child and/or as an adult. Their priorities are supported in a supplementary review of reports, policy, memoirs, and media debate. The nuance and detail in women's accounts challenge the oppositional politics of compartmentalisation and restrictions of categorisation, which inhibit the accurate reflection of experience. The subtleties within these accounts highlight the need for a social and political, rather than psychological, response that avoids pathologisation, trivialisation, or indeed sensationalism.

The approach pursued in this book prioritises women's accounts and engages critically with feminist theory and practice. Feminism is historically and practically significant as an alternative and political response to sexual violence (Jones and Cook 2008) in spite of episodic backlashes that propose its irrelevance (McRobbie 2009) and state interventions into the feminist voluntary sector that tend towards its depoliticisation (Matthews 1994; Whittier 2009). However, the processes of compartmentalisation of sexual violence as either serious or trivial, and the categorisation of 'rape

DOI: 10.1057/9781137461728.0002

victims' into credible or responsible, are challenged as they appear within the feminism of Roiphe (1993), Herman (2001), Brownmiller (1975), and MacKinnon (1995) as well as the activism of SlutWalk. Offered instead is an attempt at an ethical approach that both rejects the essentialism of the enduring and inevitably female victim, and locates trauma within the context of power dynamics and structural inequalities. Drawing from women's accounts, feminism is both critiqued and reiterated as crucial to the possibility of living differently.

Compartmentalising rape

Defining rape is both complicated and unequivocal. Academic and fieldwork definitions have changed over time and are inevitably limited. For example, within feminism, sexual violence encompasses rape, sexual assault, and childhood sexual abuse, but locating experience within structural and gendered inequalities demands the addition of a range of oppressive sexualised behaviour such as 'forced marriage, sexual harassment and stalking, trafficking and sexual exploitation, crimes of honour and female genital mutilation' (Coy et al. 2007: 4). The sex and gender of the perpetrator and 'victim' matters too. In terms of scale alone, feminism suggests it is mostly men who sexually victimise mostly girls and women. Within policy and the caring professions, though, rape and sexual violence are not gender specific but the product of faulty or disadvantaged families (Healicon 2012; Doyle 2006). Disparate definitions and explanations contribute to the compartmentalisation of sexual violence and the categorisation of the 'rape victim'. For example, within policy women who have been raped and were drunk are questionably credible (Itzin 2006), and those with unspent criminal convictions are excluded from claiming criminal injuries compensation (May and Featherstone 2011), suggesting some women are more deserving 'victims' than others.

Fundamentally, rape as it is documented in UK legislation (National Archives 2003) is the non-consensual penile penetration of the vagina, mouth, or anus. Consent, recently defined in the 2003 Sexual Offences Act, is the freedom and capacity to choose to have sex. The 'victim' is incapacitated and therefore unable to make this choice if there is violence, the threat of violence, if she is unlawfully detained, asleep or unconscious, or was unable to communicate her consent through physical disability or drugs. It is stipulated that under 16s do not have

DOI: 10.1057/9781137461728.0002

the capacity to consent. Within the confines of this specific statutory definition, there is no requirement for physical violence, or to establish the relationship between the individuals, or to evidence how they presented themselves. Ideological and practical matters obstruct cultural access to the legal definition and the embodied experience of rape. Rape mythology and victim blaming, implicit within institutional practices, obfuscate experiences of sexual violence, polarising interpretation. There is a chasm between the lived experience and the cultural articulation of rape.

For example, Marhia (2008) found the media was highly selective in its reporting of rape, with a disproportionate representation of the most violent and aggravated stranger rapes, cases leading to conviction, or rapes involving underage girls. Furthermore, rape is depicted as isolated incidents resulting from individual pathology rather than a pattern within the wider social and political context. Polarisation of experience, as a motif, demonises perpetrators and further victimises 'victims'. In the representational sphere, the malicious 'girl who cried rape' is pitted against the falsely accused and 'wronged man' (Marhia 2008). These tropes are especially prominent in the reportage of recent historical sexual abuse trials involving celebrities in the wake of the Jimmy Savile investigation, but with an additional polarisation: our more knowledgeable and proactive present is contrasted with the collusive and ignorant past. In policy, criminal justice remedies are prioritised (Phipps 2010), consequently accentuating the most recent, violent, or evidential of cases so that women who do not report are perceived as a criminal justice problem rather than requiring different services. In the sexual violence field, Lyra anticipates different responses depending on whether she is speaking of intimate partner or stranger rape.

The gap between the representation and experience of rape, evidence of the process of compartmentalisation, is similarly exaggerated within the feminism of Roiphe's (1993) early critique of the concept of 'date rape', which had catastrophic consequences for feminism's authority to define rape and 'rape victim' identity (described further in chapter two). In her article, *Date Rape's Other Victim* Roiphe (1993: np) suggests that rape has become a catch-all definition, that 'has stretched beyond bruises and knives, threats of death or violence to include emotional pressure and the influence of alcohol. The lines between rape and sex begin to blur.' Disregarding the acknowledgement of emotional coercion as a precursor to rape, as the misguided and scaremongering ideology of 'rape crisis

DOI: 10.1057/9781137461728.0002

feminists', her main concern with this 'blurring' is for date rape's other victims: those women victimised by a feminism that does not differentiate between victims of rape jokes and rape, and takes 'struggle', 'power', and 'pursuit' (Roiphe 1993: np) out of female sexuality. Moreover, to insist on the harm of 'date rape', the 'gray [sic] area in which one person's rape may be another's bad night' (Roiphe 1993: np) undermines the significance of real and 'brutal' rape. Indeed, Roiphe (1993: np) suggests, 'if we are going to maintain an idea of rape, then we need to reserve it for instances of physical violence, or the threat of physical violence'.

Although Roiphe attempts to articulate personal lived reality, which she feels is misrepresented in feminist definitions of sexual violence, her writing purposefully opposes 'bad night' and 'brutal rape'. Within both public and some feminist debates, then, the articulation of rape relies on this process of compartmentalisation, the organisation and ranking of certain behaviour and experiences through trivialisation and sensationalisation. For Mardorossian (2014) this does more than excuse the perpetrator and blame the victim, as it is only in the most exceptional and violent cases that the perpetrator-as-monster is deemed responsible. Indeed, this particular process functions to reproduce structural inequalities. Mardorossian (2014) suggests the structural, rather than biological, positions of hegemonic masculinity and feminised 'other' are imposed in rape. This reproduction of structural oppression is exacerbated in sensationalising and thereby legitimising physically violent rape as the defining experience. The gap is extended further in the trivialisation and denial of most other rape encounters. These polarised and ranked experiences lose depth and complexity (Phipps 2015), validating the gap, as alternative and nuanced experiences are excluded, but which are noticed within accounts from women:

> And you can look at it as just one person's act against one other person and I guess especially in recent years, media coverage always hones in on these very extreme cases…where it is really easy to just kind of take that individual perpetrator and really vilify them and turn them into something that is so evil and non-human and different to us as 'normal' people who don't do things like that. But really we do and it's happening all the time, everywhere to lots and lots of people. (Violet)

> There was a sort of a feeling…if it had been sink estates and working class families we wouldn't be shocked but because you are painting a picture of people that wear Marks and Spencer clothes and drink gin and tonic and go abroad on their holidays, that's messing with our heads. (Caitlin)

DOI: 10.1057/9781137461728.0002

But there was an element of somebody who you trusted doing that to you. Who then could you trust?...Whereas if it was outside, I'm not saying it's worse in or out, but in your own home where you are supposed to be safe and with my children in.... (Eliza)

...she said 'I know how you feel because I was sexually abused when I was 12', but that just made me feel awful because I thought that's so much worse than what's happened to me. (Ruby)

In these accounts women both identify, and are affected by, cultural assumptions that bear little resemblance to their experiences of rape. It is presumed sexual violence is confined to disadvantaged communities or is the product of an evil individual, and that stranger and child rape are worse than adult rape by someone known. However, in their assertion of difference from these cultural presumptions, women recognise their exclusion. In trivialisation and sensationalisation not only are these extremes of experience reduced and 'flattened out' (Phipps 2015), but women judge themselves and are ranked, silenced, and excluded from debates and services. Roiphe intended to take rape seriously, so rightly questioned the denial of an active female sexuality and the inevitability of traumatisation, themes prioritised in this book. However, in deploying compartmentalisation to argue women's responsibility and trivialise the violence of language, Roiphe reproduces rather than challenges a cultural representation of rape that precludes the material reality of women's experiences. Gay (2014: 135) challenges this insistence on the difference between the representation of rape and real experiences of rape to suggest conversely that '[w]e cannot separate violence in fiction from violence in the world no matter how hard we try.' It is not about judging severity in order to assess the legitimacy of the experience and the individual. Rather, certain language and representations are deployed to trivialise and conceal the real meaning and experience of rape, so although 'we talk about rape...we don't talk carefully about rape' (Gay 2014: 132). An ethical exploration of sexual violence is required. One that respects women's experiences without excusing the perpetrator. For Cahill (2001: 112) 'women's experiences must be articulated and respected'; otherwise, the implications of rape are more easily denied.

In an attempt to write sexual violence 'carefully', a note is required on the terminology employed in this book. As the study considers the contemporary categorisation of the 'rape victim', priority is given to women's experiences of rape that occurred on one or more occasion, at any point in their lives, as it is legally defined. Although not all participants in this study named their experiences as rape, it was agreed that 'rape' is an accurate description. However, whilst 'sexual violence' and 'childhood sexual abuse' are deployed to denote a variety of sexualised behaviour including rape imposed upon a non-consenting adult or child, when associated directly with participants these terms signify rape. This is not to obfuscate the experiences of rape, but rather to avoid repetitive writing. 'Abuse' is recognised as problematic, both obscuring the dehumanisation and objectification of a person, and acknowledging a broader range of behaviour not limited to physical violence. 'Re-victimisation' is also problematic, and when used here it denotes a pattern of systematic rape rather than suggesting that she is prone to repeated incidents. Unless otherwise stated, the perpetrator is male, and because of the way in which the cohort was recruited, all participants are female. This is not to deny sexual violence against boys and men nor the perpetration of abuse by women, but rather to recognise that within this contemporary historical and social context, sexual violence is articulated as a gendered relation.

Situating the research

Twelve women chose to become involved in this research in order to challenge the compartmentalisation of sexual violence and the categorisation of the 'rape victim' identity position. They felt their embodied reality was constrained by others' assumptions, ignorance, and judgements. Making sense of their experiences of sexual violence is a moral and ethical issue (Rowntree 2009), and in spite of the difficulties of speaking out loud, women offered to articulate publicly the nuances of their lives. Not only to counteract stereotypes and labels, but also, in providing a personal resource for those working in the field (Jordan 2008), women who participated in this research hoped to educate others in order to improve organisational response. For example, Eliza says:

> I told (my sister) that you was coming tonight and I regret saying I'd do (the interview). That was just for a moment. She said 'You're bloody stupid you. Will that make you feel any better?' so I said 'well yes it will after'. Because I feel like I might make some small contribution to help other women. Not personally for me. But it is for me, cos it makes me (feel better). Maybe if she just takes one sentence that I've said. If she takes a sentence out of what everybody says, that'll add up won't it?

DOI: 10.1057/9781137461728.0002

Eliza overcame her fear of disclosure because she wanted her account to help others feel less stigmatised. It matters to women who have experienced sexual violence and those working in the field that they are typically unheard or misconstrued; therefore, an ethical and responsible research approach is imperative. Woodward (2000) identified three significant responsibilities that became apparent as researcher of written narratives of childhood sexual abuse. Hearing personal experiences of trauma is an especially privileged position, and representing the voices of others requires not only the accurate reflection of content and meaning, but also an articulation of the researcher's agenda and methods. For, as Coffey (1999) suggests, research concerns mutuality and the co-construction of on-going interaction and interpretation. In documenting other's experiences, the researcher speaks from a position of authority, on behalf of women, and as such some discussion of her suitability to this task is required.

Woodward highlighted the importance of locating the author in the research process, but Eliza suggests another important responsibility: to make a difference in people's lives. Kelly (1988: 73) summarises it thus: feminist research insists upon, 'a commitment which includes not condoning abuse explicitly or implicitly, seeing the purpose ... as increasing understanding in order that more appropriate responses can be developed, and wanting to contribute to a long term goal of ending violence in the lives of women and children'. In recognition of the inequitable context in which sexual violence takes place, ethics demands that writing becomes 'a job of justice' (Winkler 2002: 13) that avoids sensationalising and trivialising, compartmentalising and categorising, and offers the possibility of transformation. Each of the four responsibilities identified are considered here in order to make myself visible as a reflexive researcher (Shacklock and Smyth 1998). My starting point, therefore, is to suggest my suitability for this work and my legitimacy as an intermediary are crucial to legitimate my representation of the accounts that were entrusted to me.

After years of working as a feminist activist within the UK domestic and sexual violence voluntary sector, my role in this research was primarily to facilitate the publication of nuanced experiences of sexual violence in order to realise Eliza's hope of contributing to change. I have not been raped, but my political motivation is the need to restate in different arenas experiences that are still not heard. As an intermediary, then, I could offer a practitioner's perspective and another opportunity

DOI: 10.1057/9781137461728.0002

to disseminate these alternative accounts in addition to the variety of pathways participants already utilised such as blogs and teaching as well as in their daily encounters with others.

Personal experiences could provide a researcher with a familiar connection to the participant, one that is unavailable to me and which I can only grasp vicariously. And of course morally, there are two main problems with a researcher who does not share experiences with their participants. Firstly, I cannot claim to know what rape is like, so how can I really understand something I have not experienced myself? Secondly, I aim to privilege others' accounts, but there may be occasions when my analysis is different to that offered by the participant (Fine and Weis 2010). The essence to both is a claim to truth that originates in experience that ethically requires careful consideration and prioritising. It also signifies the potential to abuse an authorial power, not rooted in experience, to make ignorant, political points. However, rather than adopt an objective and dispassionate approach that eliminates the need to acknowledge any personal interference by the researcher at all, I decided it was more ethical to celebrate co-constructed dialogue. I determined to evaluate my presumptions and continually check, refine, and review, alongside the participant, the joint research enterprise. I believe those of us who do not share these experiences are morally obliged to listen and strive to understand and identify processes and commonalities; otherwise, there is no possibility of change.

To further elucidate my role as facilitator, considered here are the interview and interpretative processes. As a practitioner in the field of sexual violence, I appreciate the privilege of hearing intimate histories. In recognition of the difficulties in speaking about experiences of sexual violence, and in order to reduce the potential distress that interviews might provoke, attempts were made to prepare participants beforehand with information about the project and myself, ensure confidentiality, and create a safe environment. Most of the participants knew me as a friend, as a colleague, or as a worker and put themselves forward for interview on that basis of prior familiarity. Others were invited to participate by their counsellor, who also knew me. Good practice guidelines were consulted and implemented (Campbell et al. 2009; 2010). For example, I was patient and respectful, and responded with warmth, compassion and understanding. I prioritised participants' emotional wellbeing. Rather than prepare questions, the participant was invited to relate her own narrative. As Woodward (2000: 39) suggests, 'what was most beneficial to my participants was the fact that I wanted to know about their experiences: I believed them, and felt that they had something valuable and worthwhile to say. I had created a space where they could tell their story.' Furthermore, as an informed and political practitioner, participants knew that I was already and unconditionally on their side and could hear and bear what they experienced as unbearable. So, all interviews were audiotaped, and transcriptions returned for comment and amendment. Maya prepared a written account instead, and we met regularly to discuss the research and my findings. Agatha and Lyra were not interviewed but contributed personal and critical comments in their on-going review of draft chapters.

The interview process felt secure and ethical because it was founded in developing relationships of mutual respect that continued through informal conversations and the sharing of transcripts and draft chapters up until publication. The longevity of these relationships facilitated the removal of the academic distinction between researcher and researched (Skinner et al. 2005). Over time as the participants became more familiar with me and the research process, confidence in their contribution and critique flourished, equalising my power as author. Indeed I was reliant on their on-going critical evaluation to verify that I had accurately heard, and represented, key themes. Drafts also provided an opportunity to engage further in debate as participants challenged, supported, or adjusted the political points I attempted to hone. Choosing particular extracts from the depth of emotive and eloquent transcripts was a difficult task, but it was informed by a combination of the priorities noted by participants, issues apparent within my work situation, and the academic and theoretical context. Out of these accounts arose the themes of trivialisation, sensationalism, categorisation, and compartmentalisation. Each quote is wonderfully expressive and simultaneously contains different sentiments, but rather than attending to every detail or emotion, I decided to pursue the prioritised theme, leaving the reader to make further considerations. Although ultimately I had authorial control, as a reflective practitioner I strove to make the research I produced remain accountable to the participants and to the field.

The purpose of this book is to make a difference in the lives of women and in fieldwork, a crucial component of feminist research. Implementing a process similar to the participatory action research spiral (Kemmis and McTaggart 2000), participants were involved in reflection, research and action, in order to effect change. Having someone take seriously their experiences reduced stigma. Reading their own transcripts, and being introduced to theory and practice responses, created opportunities to re-evaluate themselves within the context of inequalities. My role in dissemination of the research enabled the participants to connect through their narratives with other women and agencies, creating educative opportunities and raising awareness. It could be argued that change on such a small scale does not equate with the traditional notion of social transformation and that focusing on these minutiae of resistances trivialises the need for systemic social change (Kelly and Radford 1998). Indeed Bourke (2010: 430) would claim that such a focus dilutes the meaning of transformation to where 'passivity itself became a defence mechanism'. However, in a society that renders women responsible for the violence perpetrated against them, such personal and organisational transformations ought to be recognised as a significant stage of an incremental and long-term process.

The participants

It has been a privilege to hear experiences of women who volunteered to participate in this study and to have their continued support and involvement in the writing process. I did not attempt to find a representative group of women but instead relied on women putting themselves forward for interview. This felt more respectful of their decision to contribute. Rather than present life histories of each interviewee, the brief accounts provided here focus on capturing and representing the predominant feeling or concern expressed by the individual. All accounts contained elements of similar themes, but each narrative had a different emphasis, which became more apparent with each re-reading of the transcripts.

Caitlin was keen to challenge the category victim. Rather than suffer the indignity of victimhood, Caitlin engaged in the work of recovery to transform herself away from the victim in constant crisis to the unrestricted and agentic survivor in control of her life. Eliza recounted the shame she felt once she decided to report her ex-boyfriend to the police. It was imperative that Eliza should keep control of her narrative in order to prevent further encounters with shame. Amy's account focused on the difficulties of her current life. Her physical impairments and the emotional distress she often felt in the present were attributed to her experiences of childhood sexual abuse, which at the time and since have been

DOI: 10.1057/9781137461728.0002

compounded by the continuous lack of available and accessible support. Central to Donna's narrative was complicity. She felt herself responsible for two experiences of rape and two sexual assaults because at the time she had been 'stupid, drunk, and vulnerable'. Dawn felt herself diminished as a result of her experience and completed her narrative without naming the incident as rape, an issue that remained significant to her in her comments on the drafts.

Victoria was struggling with recovering memories of childhood sexual abuse which she felt prevented her from knowing the truth about what happened. Her partner Elaine also wanted some resolution to the pain of remembering, and their attempts to take back control in their lives were curtailed as outsiders within an unfamiliar culture. Ruby expressed her gratitude to all her friends and her therapist who had supported her since she was raped. Ruby was more angry towards the two men who observed her rape than towards the man who raped her, whom she refused to categorise as a rapist. Maya felt that, whilst women's organisations could deal with her 'seeking' out sexual abuse as a child, as a previously prostituted woman, in their eyes her status as victim was jeopardised. Violet's account highlighted feminism as a political tool with which to explain and reconsider her experiences of childhood sexual abuse. Agatha was concerned with the stigmatisation and perceived difference attributed to the 'rape victim', and Lyra disputed both the compartmentalisation of sexual violence and the categorisation of the 'rape victim'.

Outline of the book

The aim of this book is to provide a nuanced account of the priorities that matter to women who have experienced sexual violence. In spite of a proliferation of stories, particularly in the aftermath of the Jimmy Saville investigation, sexual violence is articulated only in formulaic proscriptions that tend to compartmentalise experience and categorise the 'victim'. It is imperative to return to women's accounts, located within systemic oppression, to provide the details and complexity, encountered in experience outside of the criminal justice system, and missing from mainstream media representation. Therefore an apparent openness to this once taboo situation in actuality has not extended society's understanding of sexual violence, and there remains a fear of disclosure. This book interrogates contemporary 'rape victim' identification from a

DOI: 10.1057/9781137461728.0002

feminist and therefore political perspective, drawing on themes important to the women interviewed. Chapters focus on identity, credibility, responsibility, and political agency. It is offered as a resource to better understand sexual violence articulated by women and to improve our responses.

Chapter 2 considers women's accounts of sexual violence to expose the contemporary categorisation of the 'rape victim' as an inherently vulnerable and careless, discreditable and tainted woman (Mardorossian 2014). Caught within shame, the individualism of therapy culture, and the oppositional politics of 'victim' and 'survivor', women describe a judged and restricted life. To offer the possibility of agency and transformation, in order to reassess subjectivity without categorisation, it is proposed that identity is not fixed and singular, but rather complicit and resistive (Foucault 1991; 2007), and emerges in ethical relations with others (Butler 2006) and within language, power, and social structures.

Chapter 3 focuses on credibility assessment as a mechanism of categorisation. In the psychological discourse of harm (O'Dell 2003) the 'rape victim' is articulated therapeutically as inevitably and enduringly damaged and stigmatised. So prolific is this discourse that it has become the measure of women's credibility and therefore their claim to truth. Within women's accounts a 'credibility conundrum' (Jordan 2004b) is identified that presents clearly the heavily policed and often impossible path to credibility. However, standing on the metaphorical cliff edge of disclosure, opportunities arise in strategies such as silence and avoidance to circumvent the inevitability of victimhood.

Chapter 4 questions victim-blaming presumptions. Originally, feminism attempted to absolve women of their responsibility but denounced their agency. Women's accounts of 'complicity', mothers' denial, and female perpetration necessitate a more robust engagement with female sexual agency particularly. Kelly's (1997a) theorisation of relative powerlessness offers an alternative that does not trivialise, sensationalise, or excuse female-perpetrated abuse, but situates female agency within differential power relations. However, women's accounts spotlight the role of others and the usually invisible perpetrator, so this theory is extended to recognise the responsibility of wider society in the reiteration of sexual violence.

Chapter 5 considers the contemporary feminist articulation of responsibility and female sexual agency in SlutWalk. Two features of neoliberalism, the risk-aware and responsible citizen (Anderson and Doherty

DOI: 10.1057/9781137461728.0002

2008) and the commodification of experience (Phipps 2015), disrupted SlutWalk's celebration of 'slut' as the essential, active female sexuality. In mainstream media feminism was blamed for sexualising young children. In feminism pro-sex and victimising feminists became entrenched and polarised positions. Therefore, returning to women's accounts of sexuality after sexual violence, it is proposed that female sexual agency is neither passive nor free, but nuanced and irreducible to the presence or absence of male sexuality.

The concluding chapter attends to the demands of feminist research to improve practice response. In order to assess the study's contribution, therefore, a summary of the concerns highlighted within women's accounts is provided, as they challenge the categorisation and essentialism of victim identity, and expose secondary harm that blames the violated woman and denies social responsibility. Evaluating this particular and careful (Gay 2014) representation of rape highlights the limitations of the research and raises further issues for practice. Recommendations for practice are suggested.

Focusing on women's accounts, the following chapters contribute to existing knowledge pertaining to the impact of sexual violence. Also offered are details and analysis of the secondary harm caused in our individual and organisational responses, in order to identify and then remedy our complicity within processes of categorisation and compartmentalisation. The summative recommendations suggest that whoever we are, when we really listen to women who have experienced sexual violence, we do so without differentiating between experiences, or assessing for credibility or harm. That we acknowledge trauma, without it becoming a defining presence, and we take seriously our responsibility to alleviate sexual violence as a manifestation and reiteration of inequality.

DOI: 10.1057/9781137461728.0002

2
Identity

Abstract: *Chapter 2 considers women's accounts of sexual violence to expose the contemporary categorisation of the 'rape victim' as an inherently vulnerable and careless, discreditable and tainted woman (Mardorossian 2014). Caught within shame, the individualism of therapy culture, and the oppositional politics of 'victim' and 'survivor', women describe a judged and restricted life. To offer the possibility of agency and transformation, in order to reassess subjectivity without categorisation, it is proposed that identity is not fixed and singular, but rather complicit and resistive (Foucault 1991; 2007) and emerges in ethical relations with others (Butler 2006) and within language, power, and social structures.*

Healicon, Alison. *The Politics of Sexual Violence: Rape, Identity and Feminism.* Basingstoke: Palgrave Macmillan, 2015. DOI: 10.1057/9781137461728.0003.

DOI: 10.1057/9781137461728.0003

You can accept what happened and it was horrible, but it didn't kill me ... it's part of what happened to me, but it is not everything that happened to me and I can't change it so I've just got to get on with it

(Agatha)

Those experiences [of childhood sexual abuse] are so kind of formative that you can't get away from it, you just can't. You know I was really young and I can't think of myself as anything, then, d'you know as someone who has suffered from abuse ... and obviously who I am as a person is kind of because of that. Or not because but that is always going to be part of it ... It's not just like, d'you know a physical pain or an emotional trauma or for whatever amount of time, but you need to kind of recognise how much it affects people's lives, (Alison: the impact) the impact it has. Having said that I would really not be happy, say somebody describing me as 'damaged'. I mean I might say it, jokingly, 'oh well, I'm damaged goods anyway' but I don't like it. Whilst I do think you have to acknowledge the impact it has, you also need to acknowledge that people do get over it and people do get on with it and it doesn't necessarily mean that you are struggling forever now. It's almost like a victimising thing, like turning you into that eternal victim when really I don't want to see myself as that. I am certainly not that anymore in any shape or form.

(Violet)

Agatha and Violet suggest that childhood sexual abuse is both horrible and formative, but assert that these particular experiences contribute to, rather than determine, their overall identity, one that continues to change and develop with time. Whilst acknowledging the impact of abuse, which in the West is perceived as inevitably and enduringly catastrophic, Agatha and Violet resist the terminology and inherent permanence of damage implicit in 'victim' categorisation. Indeed Violet infers that victimisation is not solely located in the albeit formative experience of rape necessarily, but also in the social expectations that constitute and produce the 'rape victim' as an identity position in the aftermath of rape. The need to articulate the events of sexual violence as separate from victim identification indicates two problems with the contemporary framing of the sexually violated victim: sexual violence

DOI: 10.1057/9781137461728.0003

is understood as a special kind of gendered relation that is inevitably damaging and precipitated by the inherent vulnerabilities of the female victim; and such a victimised and victimising identity position denies the possibility of female agency.

Extrapolating from the commentaries of women who have experienced sexual violence, this chapter considers Mardorossian's (2014) assertion that the sexually victimised and blamed woman is a specific and relatively recent identity categorisation. In locating this particular identity position within the contemporary cultural context, Mardorossian challenges the essentialism of the 'rape victim' as inevitably and deficiently female to promote instead a subject who is structurally rather than biologically derived. In so doing she severs the presumed link between the 'rape victim's' vulnerabilities and her responsibility for rape, and offers the possibility of female agency. However, just as Agatha and Violet suggest, the appropriation of 'rape victim' as an identity position in its current configuration is problematic as it galvanises the operation of category construction that delimits women's lives. In order to critically engage with categorisation of the 'rape victim', then, rather than pursue the psychological notion of the inevitably fixed and damaged individual, the aim here is to consider a range of theories that emphasise intersubjectivity. Supplementing the work of Mardorossian, it is argued that rape victim identity is an intersubjective categorisation, constituted within the intra-actions of bodies, social spaces, structures, language, and matrices of power where distinct practices are deployed to monitor and regulate. Intersubjectivity therefore signifies the importance of rape, not as a women's issue or of concern to specific women, but to society as a whole (Mardorossian 2014). Furthermore, acknowledging human interdependence as fundamental to normative existence demands a more ethical relation with the other (Butler 2004), and this has implications for practice and political transformation.

Identity in accounts of sexual violence

The following accounts, from interviews with women who have experienced sexual violence, convey meaning in excess of that extricated for the purposes of this argument and have been selected because they communicate particularly contradictory and competing ideas about the contemporary articulation of the 'rape victim' as a specific identity

DOI: 10.1057/9781137461728.0003

position. Together the impact of sexual violence is clearly demonstrable. Additional excerpts have been identified in each section.

I am not just this broken, fragmented person, I am a human being.... Because it would just be this emptying out, wouldn't it, of, well it would be a world view of being defined by what's happened to me, rather than I existed before any of it happened to me. (Caitlin)

it's hard to live a normal life because you kind of think you are not normal. (Elaine)

I remember telling somebody and she said 'oh and you're so normal' ... What do people think you are going to be and it is so common, you probably know three other women who 'are normal'. (Agatha)

There is always going to be a difference between your friends who haven't had that experience. (Ruby)

What happens when rape ... or abuse happens, you feel your body betrays you ... you are cut off from your body, cut off from your anger. (Elaine)

(the police officer) asked if she could interview the children (as they had been in house when she was raped), and I said 'no you can't.' I said 'I want them to have a childhood ... I don't want them thinking of their mum in that way.' (Eliza)

And that's another thing, don't ever call me a survivor or a victim. I hate both of those words it makes me feel even weaker. I did get out of the situation but I got out of the situation in a very passive way.... These labels should not be used to define us, because of a single (or multiple life event) ... I am first a human being and then a woman, a lesbian, a civil partner, a lover, a daughter, sister, aunt, almost a mother, a carer, a friend. I am all these things and many more and in no particular order, because it is the sum of whom I am that defines me as unique. (Dawn)

It just changed who I was.... I felt really pathetic and you know that victim thing. (Ruby)

And the sense of respect that I get from her is not 'poor you, all the things you've been through'. It's survivor in the right sense of the word. I think what an amazing resilience that you have to survive all of that and be working through this now and I think that's the positive use of the word survivor isn't it, that when you realise that it is life endangering events that we have survived, that just being alive is an achievement. But just because you've achieved that it doesn't mean you can't go and achieve more. (Caitlin)

Because if you are a victim and life is shit, it always will be. Well we might as well give up and go home straightaway, hadn't we? I think that is worse than the original abuse, isn't it? Because whatever happens to us, the awful

DOI: 10.1057/9781137461728.0003

stuff that happened to me…. That can't determine my life. It is what I am doing now that determines it, my choices that determine my life, isn't it? I think that's too much within that kind of discourse of the victim. (Caitlin)

we have to look at it in the context of the system we live in which is kind of restricting the way we can kind of think about things, or the terms you use and people try to overcome it but it is really difficult to break out of that. (Violet)

The dehumanising and objectifying process of sexual violence is 'an attempt to murder our identity (Winkler 2002: 36), to shatter and redefine 'out of existence' the victim's sense of self (Brison 2002: 45). In these excerpts women speak of being broken and fragmented, of losing themselves, of suffering irreparable damage, and feeling disconnected from their bodies. In the perpetrator's denial of corporeal boundaries, she becomes dispossessed of her body and mind, and differentiated from the 'normal'. Brison and Winkler articulate this difference, as being branded, stigmatised, victimised: For example, Brison (2002: 49) suggests that, 'such an attempt [to distance one's self from the degradation] is never wholly successful and the survivor's bodily sense of self is permanently altered by an encounter with death that leaves one feeling 'marked' for life'. Similarly, Winkler (2002: 100) observes that '[f]riends have defined [her] now as rape traumatised and tattooed emotionally, and those branded marks of pain, for them, would remain forever. The attack permeated all of [her] existence, or so they thought, and left everything about [her] damaged.' Infiltrated by his violence, she is contaminated, isolated in her difference and her potential to contaminate others.

It is clear from these excerpts that the destruction of the self in sexual violence occurs, and is reproduced, in relationships and connections with others. As noted in Winkler's comment, it is her friends, family, and supporters who sustain the belief in the permanence of stigmatisation. For Bourke (2010: 7), '[r]apists literally invade and attempt to conquer the sexual terrain of their victims, and through transforming her 'no' into a 'yes' strive to triumph over their social territory too.' Whilst Brison (2002) would argue that certain community is nurturing and necessary for healing, in the above excerpts where demands are made to be recognised as human, social proscription is rejected. Labelling, categorisation, and the resultant expectations are resisted as a further form of violence. Identity descriptors such as survivor and victim are deployed in the writing of Brison, Winkler, and Bourke with particular purpose, to articulate the devastation caused and the effort required in recovery.

DOI: 10.1057/9781137461728.0003

But the excerpts expose such terminology especially as problematic in its insistence on categorisation.

The need to avoid categorisation is reasonable though, given that the 'rape victim' is framed within contemporary Western culture as a blameworthy woman. Mardorossian (2014) argues that previously 'victim' referred to a person affected by tragic or criminal event(s) beyond and unconnected to the individual's psyche. However recently, victimhood, epitomised in the 'rape victim', has come to denote a woman who, due to her own carelessness or inherent vulnerability, is weak, overwhelmed, or manipulated by an external source. Moreover, despite his perpetration, it is the 'victim' who becomes the repository of taint and responsibility. As an identity position, then, Mardorossian suggests that the 'rape victim' is not a fixed categorisation but one that is constituted within particular social and historical contexts. Whilst Mardorossian is not suggesting a fluid or fleeting subjectivity either, she does engage with identity as disentangled from the biologically sexed body. The anti-essentialism pursued by Mardorossian is considered here as it offers the possibility of female agency and change whilst acknowledging a subjectivity tied to, but not fixed within, social structures. Agency and change, as noted in the accounts, are important themes for women whose lives are circumscribed by this categorisation.

Mardorossian (2014) suggests that contemporarily, the passive, weak, and inevitably female rape victim is constituted in opposition to the valorised autonomous, self-possessed, and agentic male. Unlike other theories, which propose the gendered binary causes sexual violence in the expression and enactment of aggressive masculinity and victimised femininity, Mardorossian suggests that sexual violence sustains this gendered polarity. She argues that an insatiable will to dominate defines hegemonic masculinity and requires repeated performances of supremacy through acts of violence since the dominance of masculinity is only ever achieved and confirmed in the feminisation and subjugation of the other. However, the subject position of hegemonic masculinity and feminised other are structurally rather than biologically derived. That is, Mardorossian (2014: 3) suggests that 'dominant masculinity can be occupied by either men or women, while structural femininity is a position that may define and subordinate men, minorities, and other marginalised groups just as effectively as it does the category women'. These acts of violence are not necessarily sexually violent per se, but by virtue of the event affirming the masculinity of the perpetrator and

DOI: 10.1057/9781137461728.0003

the feminisation of the subjugated other, it is sexualised violence. As Mardorossian suggests (2014: 17), it is not the case that every form of violence is rape 'but that rape is paradigmatic form all violation takes in a culture where all violence is sexualised and where normative subjectivity is produced through a reliance on an economy of dominance and violation'. Although the gendered binary is separated from the biological body, it requires sexualised acts of violence to sustain it. Therefore, in the insistence of the centrality of the will to dominate in hegemonic masculinity, sexual violence is intrinsic to the formation of gendered and other marginalised subject positions.

Mardorossian asserts the primacy of rape in the constitution of race, class, and gender to offer a theorisation that prioritises a relational identity and recognises the necessity of a political response. If, as Mardorossian suggests, sexual violence reproduces the gendered binary through the imposition of dominance of hegemonic masculinity and structural femininity in sexualised acts of violence, then the contemporary rape victim identity has significant implications for living a 'life that counts' (Butler 2004). Firstly, contemporary rape victim identity is sustained both by its historicity and a kind of contemporary momentum. Secondly, the presentation of the gendered self, and the 'rape victim' especially, is severely restricted; and thirdly, articulating agency, especially a gendered agency, within structural and discursive limits is possible but remains experientially and theoretically problematic. Whilst Mardorossian situates the inevitability of the female rape victim within this particular historical and cultural context, and decouples victimhood from women and dominance from men, the presentation of this categorisation, and female agency, require further consideration. The restrictions and resistances to rape victim identity as a categorisation constituted relationally within this specific social and historical context are explored in relation to themes identified from within women's accounts.

Dissociated and damaged

> [Childhood sexual abuse or rape] changes who you are. And maybe you
> have a memory of who you were before and it's really silly to think that you
> can just be who you were before because you cannot be. But if you have a
> memory of who you were before and you want to get back to yourself, get
> pieces of yourself together ... you will have a question 'who am I?' and 'what
> do I want to do with this?' (Elaine)

DOI: 10.1057/9781137461728.0003

The notion that identity is singular, rational, and fixed is challenged within accounts from women who describe their experiences of sexual violence in terms of dissociation, a feeling of separation from the incidents, the body, and memories. The traumatised and splintered self offers an opportunity to reconsider subjectivity that incorporates resistance to categorisation that defines and delimits the rape victim as 'damaged'. Drawing on Furedi's (2004) exposition of therapy culture, this section considers identity in its contemporary expression to explore the limits of psychology as the defining discourse for understanding the construction of the self and the 'rape victim' in particular. Foucault's (1991) theorisation of 'disciplinary power' is then considered to further identify the constitution of the subject within particular and contradictory discourse and relations of power that privilege certain knowledge and practice. In order to pursue the possibility of agency, Foucault's (2007) 'acts of freedom' are also considered in relation to a gendered normative subjectivity as it is constructed in the dominance of hegemonic masculinity and structural femininity.

In the excerpts above, dissociation, intrusive memories, and paralysing fear have come to signify an identity position that solidifies with every response and imposition of cultural expectation. The entanglement of the self in relation to others in a process to 'rape victim' identification is apparent in Brison's (2002: 8) description of the forensic examination that took place after she was raped: 'For about an hour the two of them went over me like a piece of meat, calling out measurements of bruises and other assessments of damage, as if they were performing an autopsy. This was just the first of many incidents in which I felt as if I was experiencing things posthumously.' In the dehumanising attack Brison was left for dead, her sense of self shattered and dissociated, but these encounters with metaphorical death in others' responses affirm and reproduce dehumanisation and dissociation, leaving her continually doubting who she was. Professionals – doctors, psychiatrists, academics, legislators – categorise the self, arbitrarily define, assess, and monitor according to cultural standards of normality (Burman 2003) or behaviour expected of the rape victim (Warner 2003). Her interpretation or presence is not necessarily required. In categorisation, the individual affects of sexual violence are re-articulated in psychological terminology, the primary sense-making rhetoric. Expression of violation, therefore, is not testament to social injustice, but psychological problems she has to manage. However, it is apparent in the excerpts above that this framing

DOI: 10.1057/9781137461728.0003

of rape victim identity is contested. For Brison and others, the destruction caused in the aftermath of rape necessitates rethinking identity as a fixed reality and especially in relation to others within the culturally accepted explanatory framework of psychology.

In contemporary Anglo-American societies, Furedi (2004) argues, therapeutic culture has become the most important signifier of meaning in everyday life. The proliferation of therapeutic culture occurred alongside the neoliberal preoccupation with individualism, risk, and responsibility, at a time when individuals are severed from strong ideological commitments to communities and politics, and uncertainties in life are transformed into high risk encounters. As such, Furedi suggests, structural inequalities are explained away as personalised, psychological problems; everyone is positioned as vulnerable; and everyday situations are turned into tests of emotional resilience. Despite the appearance of self-enhancement, therapeutic culture in actuality impoverishes and denigrates the individual. Furedi (2004: 21) claims that the therapeutic imperative

> posits the self in distinctly fragile and feeble form and insists that the management of life requires the continuous intervention of therapeutic expertise, therefore, therapeutic culture has helped construct a diminished sense of self that characteristically suffers from an emotional deficit and possesses a permanent consciousness of vulnerability. Its main legacy, so far, is the cultivation of a unique sense of vulnerability.

This diminished self is personified in the concept of the victim. Legitimate emotions are pathologised, people identify themselves through their illness, and virtuous disclosure marks the management of people's emotions. Therapeutic culture not only produces vulnerability, but it justifies particular interventions. Counselling provides meaning but only because it is subsumed within a therapeutic ethos embodied in social institutions.

The project of the self as a contemporary priority has been debated widely, and although Furedi only alludes to sexual violence, the therapeutic construction and 'treatment' of the diminished self is clearly relevant to the recent framing of the 'rape victim'. His criticism suggests a particular enclosed and self-fulfilling societal imperative that not only creates and sustains victims but forecloses any alternative mode of understanding. More specifically, Furedi's analysis of therapeutic culture suggests the rape victim is situated within localised discursive practices.

DOI: 10.1057/9781137461728.0003

Whereas previously, women might express their distress as physically and economically ruinous (Clark 1987), Bourke (2010) contends that within therapeutic culture the act of sexual violation has become an identity position entirely articulated as devastating psychologically. However, Furedi's critique is primarily motivated to highlight his concern that therapeutic culture justifies state intervention into the private sphere. Implicating feminism in this process, he argues that the home is increasingly promoted as dangerous particularly for women and children, and everyday conflict is recast as abuse, turning routine experience into a source of emotional distress. In spite of this trivialisation of feminist praxis, it is useful to extrapolate from two of Furedi's points. Firstly, psy-science established itself as the authority and primary definer of childhood sexual abuse and rape, eliminating both alternative explanatory approaches and political engagement with power and control. And secondly, given that these discursive practices are historically and culturally located, there are opportunities for change and resistance.

Furedi blames feminism for the displacement of attention away from public behaviour to private, internalised identities, compounding the exclusion of alternative critiques, and provoking societal depoliticisation. However, O'Dell (2003) suggests feminism is implicated differently, in the proliferation and conservatism of the therapeutic imperative. For O'Dell, feminism's original theorisation of sexual violence as a manifestation of patriarchal power was instrumental in political and collective responses that were discredited and sidelined as psy-science claimed expertise in the 1970s. Rather than operating to foreclose other discursive practices, feminism was the excluded radical alternative, a process that also involved transformation of feminist organisations through state funding obligations and restrictions (Jones and Cook 2008). Moreover, in order to legitimate the seriousness of sexual violence, feminism adopted the psychological model of trauma (albeit problematically). In the appropriation of therapeutic language, exemplified in feminist therapy, that required individual rather than social change and recognition of the psychologically damaged but innocent victim, Becker (2005) suggests feminism relinquished its political impetus. The move away from political action to therapy, along with the assumed feminist insistence that all women are victims (Roiphe 1993), fuelled a backlash that accused feminism of victimising. According to Mardorossian (2014) the political correctness discourse of the 1990s further delimited the victim as one who rejects that status. Victimhood no longer signified innocence.

DOI: 10.1057/9781137461728.0003

Rather, its taint necessitated immediate disconnection, and significantly within feminist praxis 'survivor' became the preferred identity. Within this contemporary therapy culture then, feminism was sidelined and accused of creating victims, individual identity management was prioritised above social and political action, and together, the 'rape victim' became entrenched as a stigmatised identity.

Furedi was clear about the dangers of therapy as a practice and discourse to the contemporary manifestation of the self. For women who have experienced sexual violence, this framing of the rape victim is particularly limiting, but not totalising, as it is located within a specific history and context that suggests the possibility of change. In his conception of 'disciplinary power' (1991) and ethical practice (2007) Foucault offers a theorisation of historically and culturally located subjectivity that accommodates both profound limitations and opportunities for agency. Foucault's self emerges by virtue of inhabiting and incorporating social norms legitimated within matrices of power and truth that are invested in discursive fields. The self is not an established core that exists prior to action, but instead is borne out of perpetual (re)invention through practices that are simultaneously constraining and transforming. Foucault (1991: 177) describes constraining and disciplinary power as that which is not 'possessed as a thing, or transferred as a property; it functions like a piece of machinery.' Disciplinary power is exercised pervasively, silently through observation, detailed scrutiny, and constant surveillance. Whilst disciplinary power operates discreetly, the constantly observed are brought out into the open and therefore maintained in their subjection. Through documentation such as case notes, the subject becomes objectified in codes and classifications, which Foucault (1991: 190) suggests is 'the first stage of "formalisation" of the individual in power relations'. Certain knowledge is privileged and taken up as truth. So, Mardorossian's rape victim, constituted within disciplinary power and established truths of science, medicine, and policy, is recognised, defined, and categorised, but her visibility requires that she is monitored and treated.

Alongside the more obvious and punitive operations of power Foucault (2007: 154) suggests there are 'technologies of the self' which 'permit individuals to perform, by their own means, a certain number of operations on their own bodies, on their own souls, on their own thoughts, on their own conduct, and this in such a way that they transform themselves, modify themselves and reach a certain state of perfection, of happiness,

DOI: 10.1057/9781137461728.0003

of purity'. Such technologies, exemplified in confession or psy-science, inculcate compliance, an abdication of state responsibility, as individuals participate in their own regulation. However, Foucault also offers an ethical self-transformation that challenges the boundaries of knowledge and truth but remains contained within the permissible. 'Acts of freedom' as ethical practice extend or critique social norms. Rather than revolutionise discourse, though, within matrices of power and truth, Foucault (2007: 45) asserts ethical practice is necessarily 'the art of not being governed quite so much'. Drawing from Foucault's theorisation of subjectivity, therefore, the 'rape victim' emerges within discursive practices and relations of power that are both obvious and self-actualising. Constraints and limitations are not totalising but ambivalently negotiated.

Furedi and Foucault provide tools with which to consider the (re)formation of 'rape victim' identity within contemporary administrative, therapeutic, and scientific neoliberalism where sexual behaviour and identity are subsumed. It could be argued that Furedi's polemic details the implications of therapy as a technology of the self, whilst Foucault's wider theorisation encompasses the constitution of subjectivity within the operation of power and truth. Proposing identity as relational and ambivalent, rather than fixed and determined by the social norms of the specific historical context, Foucault and Furedi facilitate the possibility of agency and social change important to Mardorossian. It is not that an autonomous subject has Rape Culture imposed on her. Instead the 'rape victim' emerges within matrices of power and privileged truth, an ambivalent relation involving negotiation and critique. Moreover, it is worth noting that gendered power relations are further constructed within codes of morality which, Foucault (1997: 263) suggests, involve distinguishing 'between the code that determines which acts are permitted or forbidden and the code that determines the positive or negative value of the different possible behaviours'. To live a life that counts, the individual does not only abide by the codes that determine what is permissible but in relation to the value placed upon these authorised behaviours. Encountered on this narrow path to a liveable life is shame which further evidences the significance of relational identity. Hegemonic masculinity necessitates the subjugation of the other epitomised in sexual violence and becomes re-inscribed in practices that affirm and reproduce dehumanisation of the 'rape victim'. Consideration of shame suggests that is not a simple acceptance.

DOI: 10.1057/9781137461728.0003

Different and contaminated

> I felt that it had affected me irreparably, psychologically, you know, and I used to worry if I have children, will I have issues that I will just pass onto my children. (Ruby)

> you don't want to tell anyone, because people have the idea that 'oh people who have been abused, become, they abuse people don't they'. (Agatha)

> I feel like I am being tortured, eaten and swallowed and tortured again by shame. All the memories about everything come back...and I can't switch it off.... With fear it is easier to deal with, an anxiety attack can be talked through, but shame is excruciating. (Victoria)

It has been argued so far that the negligent and enduring female 'rape victim' is a culturally and historically specific identity position. Contemporary morality is reiterated through discursive practices constituted in the 'rape victim', who is revealed as inherently flawed. In the previous excerpts this flaw, and the possibility that her badness could be exposed, is expressed as difference and contamination. Much like Goffman's (1963: 11) still relevant 'discreditable identity', women's accounts suggest that great effort is required to manage situations and information about their failing, so that this flaw, not immediately perceptible to others, remains undiscovered. The fear of being found deficient or of contaminating others is not only severely limiting but makes shame a primary possibility. Shame is further compounded in a society which is affronted by the intimate and sexual manifestation of power in sexual violence and privileges particular knowledge that presumes the cycle of abuse. However, whilst shame feels excruciating, it functions at a fundamental level to connect the individual with society. Indeed, for Probyn (2000a), disgust and shame ought to be recognised, not for the paralysis they induce, but for the disruption they can cause to a culture of blame. Mindful of the above excerpts, the writing on shame of Ahmed (2004), Bartky (1990), Guenther (2012), and Probyn (2000a; 2000b) is considered to explore this intersubjectivity that necessitates a re-evaluation of identity not as essentially gendered, but rather as the presentation and critique of contemporary morality that holds the possibility for change.

Indicative of contemporary morality and relevant to this discussion on shame is the cycle of abuse theory, a predominant and influential explanation for both the perpetration of sexual violence and re-victimisation. This theory, encompassed in national policy in the UK and accepted widely in practice, suggests sexual violence is attributable to an impoverished or abusive childhood that renders deficient the identity of the 'victim', resulting in a gendered reproduction of abuse. Boys go onto perpetrate violence, whilst girls continue the pattern of repeated victimisation. Furthermore, whilst abused men are excused of their perpetrating behaviour, victimised women are held responsible for their re-victimisation. Furedi (2004) is particularly critical of the inevitability of abuse as permanently damaging because he fears this discourse justifies state intervention into the private sphere. However, a more ambivalent relationship to inevitable damage is suggested in the above excerpts, and shame is central to appreciating both the acceptance of and resistance to stigmatisation. Supplementing the framing of the careless and blameworthy rape victim, the cycle of abuse theory not only taps into, but authorises the shame that women feel and – combined with the hatred contained in the perpetrator's words, deeds, and thoughts – infiltrates her mind and body in sexual violence. She feels contaminated and, although she attempts to conceal the stigmatisation, she feels branded, an obvious and targetable victim. She fears she contaminates (children) through behaviour that others may deem inappropriate, with the badness that she conceals and cannot expel nor contain. She fears she might traumatise others in the words and images she employs to articulate who she has become. Moreover, if it is not expelled or controlled, then this latent contaminant could jeopardise any future relations with others. Shame therefore involves a painful and critical reappraisal of self in relation to the judgements of others and a contemporary social morality that supports rape mythology.

In his classic phenomenology, Sartre (2003) suggests that shame is bound up with how the self feels about itself, a sense of personal inadequacy and failure, experienced usually before an actual or idealised other. This feeling of exposure introduces something irreversible into the self's perception of itself. In light of the exposure the self is renegotiated in relation to how the other beholds it, 'passing judgement' on itself as an object as it appears to the other, therefore grasping knowledge of itself through the medium of the other. In shame the self recognises itself as it is seen by others, a 'being-for-others' which challenges how the self was originally regarded and contests the position of mastery of the self of itself. The exposed self does not have immediate access to its appearance in the moment, unlike the seeing and knowing external other, and so the self is transformed in recognition of the other's judgement. Sartre (2003: 296)

DOI: 10.1057/9781137461728.0003

describes this double movement as such: 'I am ashamed *of* myself *before* the Other.' For Ahmed (2004: 104), unlike pain and disgust,

> [t]he bind of shame is that it is intensified by being seen by others as shame. The bad feeling which in pain is related to the object, in shame it is attributed to oneself. In disgust the subject gets filled up by something bad but this badness gets expelled and sticks to the bodies of others, but in shame, I feel myself to be bad and so to expel the badness, I have to expel myself from myself. In shame, the subject's movement back into itself is simultaneously a turning away from itself in shame. The subject may have nowhere to turn.

The excerpts above demonstrate the intensity of shame and Sartre's account elucidates the internalisation of society's negativity and disapproval, to suggest shame is potentially deeply disempowering. But as Guenther (2012: 61) argues, shame 'intersubjectifies; it attests to an irreducible relation to others in the midst of one's own self-relation. However painful shame may be, it confirms this relationality of the subject, and could not arise without it.' In this interrelation shame both exposes and challenges contemporary morality. Before detailing shame's relationality, considered here is the possibility that shame, in its ambivalence, is productive.

For Bartky (1990) shame is not only profoundly disempowering but affects women particularly. Regardless of shameful encounters, the presumption of an equality that is in fact absent causes an inherent inadequacy in women that produces shame. Indeed for Bartky (1990: 98) shame compounds the oppression of women in that 'the oppressed must struggle not only against more visible disadvantages, but against guilt and shame as well. The experience of shame may tend to lend legitimacy to the structure of authority that occasions it.' Similarly Ahmed suggests the shame that is felt in the failure to live up to an ideal is a way of taking up and internalising that ideal. Despite the need to negate the feelings left by shame, it confirms a love for, and commitment to, such ideals in the first place and shame's necessary place in moral development, since shame is an acceptance of society's censure. Ahmed (2004: 106) suggests that 'shame is the affective cost of not following the scripts of normative existence.... The role of shame is therefore to secure the (hetero)normative.' Shame produces an agonising yet authentic conformity which for Bartky is detrimental to women. For Ahmed, however, excruciating conformity suggests an equivocation, both compliance and resistance, that is potentially productive.

DOI: 10.1057/9781137461728.0003

Feminist identity politics and pride movements such as Reclaim The Night and SlutWalk provide opportunities to challenge the visible disadvantages of oppression Bartky identifies through the reclamation of shame. For Probyn (2000b: 128) '[t]he logic of pride movements reproduces an antagonism between "us" the shamed and "them" the guilty. This is especially effective when bodies who have been shamed group en masse to return the shaming epithets: "shame at your attitudes – feel guilt at your aversion."' Whilst Furedi's (2004) criticism of identity politics concerns the recognition of pain and shame as reproducing a diminished and fragile subjectivity, Probyn (2000a: 128) argues that '[s]uch tactics … bypass any individual avowal and recognition of disgust.' The problem with pride movements is not that they celebrate the shamed subject but rather the need to transform and relinquish shame immediately forecloses detailed analysis of shameful events, leaving the guilty admonished rather than shamed. Feeling guilty is not productive. Probyn (2000a: 57) suggests that shame can be employed,

> as a switching point re-routing the dynamics of knowing and ignorance. Unlike empathy, shame does not permit any automatic sharing of commonality, it is that which poses deep limits to communication. Shame can be made to insist on the specific nature of the acts that caused it: it can be made to mark the awesome materiality of its own condition a possibility.

Relating Probyn's argument to sexual violence specifically, the radical potential of shame, therefore, lies in the details. Detailing disgust and analysing shame exposes the perpetrator's strategies and secrets to problematise the categorising of the disgusting and the actions of those who position others as disgusting. Shame is productive because it causes us to acknowledge that it is the perpetrators and rape supporters who are shameful. Perpetrators unable to circumvent shame are motivated to reflect on their actions.

Examination of perpetrator strategies that induce shame is fundamental in challenging stigma and difference, as is locating the onus of sexual violence with the perpetrators and questioning societal excuses. However, Guenther's (2012) article particularly resonates with shame in sexual violence because she focuses on the intimacy of the interrelationship between the oppressed and the oppressor. Even in situations where perpetrators lack shame and refuse to accept responsibility, or society exonerates their actions, Guenther suggests that her shame keeps open the possibility that things could be different. Indeed she emphasises

DOI: 10.1057/9781137461728.0003

shame as the mark of being human, a resistance to the dehumanising other rather than an excruciating conformity to social values. For Guenther (2012: 64) 'the capacity for shame attests to a remnant, however small, of interhuman relationality . . . . This is why shame can function as a site of resistance, a feeling for justice even in the midst of radical injustice: because it confirms the root of responsibility in our relations with others.' This indestructible humanity is defined not by subjectivity but in the process of difference. Guenther (2012: 70) suggests that

> this alterity can be violated, denied, degraded – but it can never be utterly destroyed, because it cannot help addressing itself to the other whom it seeks to annihilate . . . . Thus subjectification occurs *in spite* of the project of desubjectification . . . . In order to desubjectify you, they still have to single you out, and in singling you out, they undermine the very project of effacing your singularity.

In sexual violence, shame signifies resistance to the absolute attempt at dehumanisation. In the very process of degradation, the subject-other is reaffirmed and her shame testifies to this defiance which in its detailing and the politics of pride movements becomes a more collective move to justice. Although this theorisation of shame suggests this aspect of subjectification is constituted in the inhumanity of another – that is, in this instance, identity is defined in relation to the persecutor – the 'project of desubjectification' articulates the process of sexual violence described in women's accounts. However, Guenther's insistence on the significance of an indestructible humanity defined in processes of difference, rather than in essential subjectivity, offers the possibility that shame both presents and challenges contemporary morality and the social values that condone sexual violence. It also offers the possibility of understanding shame as both acceptance and rejection of difference since stigmatisation is borne out of degradation and resistance.

Victim and survivor

> I still hate this description [of survivor] for all sorts of reasons not least because it just doesn't make sense to me. What exactly have we survived? Life? And can labelling yourself a 'survivor' really be a source of pride to counteract the shame? (Violet)
>
> This makes me wonder about my attitude to disclosure. I still feel strongly that I should disclose, that I should be transparent and open ('be the change

DOI: 10.1057/9781137461728.0003

that you want to see in the world'), that it is a political act. However, does it actually benefit me or others? Does it change the situation? Is it worth it? Or does it just lead to me continuously reaffirming the object/victim status? (Violet)

In sexual violence shame necessitates the recognition of a contaminated identity as it is judged within social norms and morality that presume women's culpability. However, in the intimacy of violation, shame also signifies defiance, and subsequent disclosure exposes the perpetrator's wrong-doing, creating opportunities not only for individual retribution but also social change. Identity politics support the process to justice but often subscribe to the cultural obligation to accept victim positioning in order to either facilitate recovery or promote difference and equality, and for Mardorossian, the classification of victim is so tainted it requires immediate transformation. Outlined in the excerpts above, and within feminism, victim-survivor categorisation is contested. This debate is considered here because it matters that women claim neither to be victims nor survivors of sexual violence, defying the operation of erasure and legitimation that identity categorisation involves, and this has implications for practice. The victim-survivor binary is examined in relation to Butler's (2006) notion of cultural intelligibility, as it describes the demarcation of a liveable life. Butler also offers a theorisation with which to reconsider categorisation altogether, and therefore challenge the essentialist duality of subjugated femininity and hegemonic masculinity that is sustained in sexual violence as noted by Mardorossian. It has been argued that subjectivity is the reiteration and rejection of cultural categorisation within social interrelationships, exemplified in the shame of sexual violence, and Butler suggests that when we recognise our interdependence as it is exposed in loss and vulnerability, a shared ethical and political project begins.

It has been previously suggested that as psy-science claimed expertise within the sexual violence field, feminism appropriated the terminology of victim to convince the public and professionals of the seriousness of the trauma rape produced and testify to innocence and truth within women's experiences. However, categorisation of the pathologised rape victim is problematic, not only in the depoliticisation of a social issue and the assertion of passivity, but in the construction of an entire establishment that constrains and reproduces this diminished identity position. To verify that sexual violence took place, and to determine the severity of it, an individual is expected to manifest trauma proportionately. To

DOI: 10.1057/9781137461728.0003

be recognised as innocent, therefore, agency is relinquished, victimhood accepted, and recovery secured; otherwise, the risk is social castigation. Indeed after Natascha Kampusch escaped from being held captive in 2006, public response soon turned antipathetic because she defied victimhood conventions (Van Dijk 2009). Questioning terminology, Lamb (1999) argues that 'victim' is overused and doubly controversial. If elements of feminism suggest all women by virtue of membership to an oppressed group are victims, then the term does no justice to victims of abuse. Simultaneously, there occurs an over-purifying of victims so that only the very tortured are entitled to claim victim identification. Lamb's solution to the inherent passivity of victimhood, and to emphasise the 'specialness' of sexual victimisation, is to recognise agency in the responsibility that women own in sexual violence. For when others ignore her assertion of fault and insist she is blameless, it presumes they know more about her agency than she does. It is deeply troubling that women are assessed as real or fake, and that professionals think they know more than the individual about 'rape victim' identity or, indeed, that there is a perceived difference between professionals and 'victims'. However, rather than accept victim blaming implicit in the prioritisation of her responsibility, it is argued here that the process to categorisation requires interrogation theoretically and practically. For the rape victim is not the only problematic identity position.

'Survivor' is perceived as the better proposition as it signifies agency, defiance, and progress. Especially as Mardorossian (2014) suggests the 'rape victim' is no longer defined in relation to innocence alone and has become further delineated as disreputable, negligent, and stigmatised, an identity position that necessitates immediate dissociation. That is, to identify with, rather than as, a victim is preferable. However, in an online blog, Lyra (2014) argues that 'survivor' is similarly encumbered in its inevitable connection with dehumanising incident(s) and because it implies an inherent bravery rejected by women who feel they have been complicit, collusive, or passive (as Violet and Dawn suggest in the above excerpts). Of particular concern for Lyra (2014: np) though, is the definitive and swift recovery:

> it still shocks me the extent to which there's a palpable shift in my relationship with some women, where the way in which they speak to and look at me has fundamentally changed. The pressure to 'transform', to 'become a survivor', to go to counselling and stop talking about it in such an uncomfortable, angry, raw and realistic way has been extreme. It feels as

DOI: 10.1057/9781137461728.0003

though there's something so stigmatised about the idea of being a victim that women must instantly transform – 'make something good' out of our suffering, 'move on'.

If, and that's a huge if, we are ever able to speak about our own experiences 'as professionals', we must be 'survivors'. We must have learnt and grown, and ultimately realised what we could do better.

Survivor identity may suggest a more dynamic subjectivity, but Lyra is confronted with social demands to transform away from the stigmatised victim into the dutiful survivor, no longer troublesome, but contained, managed (Warner 2003), and prerequisite of professional practice. Survivor identity then, for Lyra, functions to both sanitise sexual violence and harm women's relationships with other women. In her recovery, the survivor is cleansed of the horror; she is tracked and monitored and provided with personal strategies protecting others from such knowledge and distress. This 'recovered' survivor is pitted against other women who, according to Lyra, 'haven't gone through this "process" in the way we perceive has been helpful for us to feel better'. Considering the consequences of a 'them and us' approach, Lyra asks (2014: np): 'How do we face the knowledge that some women don't really feel better? Do we blame them? "Teach" them how to become "survivors" or "thrivers" like us?'

Lyra's critique of survivor categorisation highlights three significant and interrelated themes. Firstly, compartmentalising rape into opposing experiences conceals an implicit and symbolic violence that operates within language. According to Zizek (2009: 52) the symbolic violence of language is, in its simplification of the thing, 'reducing it to a single feature. It dismembers the thing, destroying its organic unity, treating its parts and properties as autonomous. It inserts the thing into a field of meaning which is ultimately external to it.' That is, in its capacity to define, language is inherently violent because essential truths (of the thing or indeed identity) are diminished or destroyed and can only be made meaningful within discursive constraints. Zizek (2009: 57) suggests there is also a 'fantasmatic dimension' to language which further delimits, in this case, the articulation of abuse. The fantasy of the 'innocent' victim overdetermines the way in which this identity position is perceived by the individual and others. So universal is the fantasy image that it exerts a 'performative efficiency'. To paraphrase Zizek (2009: 62), 'it is not merely an interpretation of what [victims of sexual violence] are, but an interpretation that determines the very being and social existence of the interpreted subjects.' 'Innocence' as it is expected within contemporary

DOI: 10.1057/9781137461728.0003

mores and norms, contained in categorisation determines the existence of the 'rape victim' and 'survivor'. The antagonism of the victim-survivor binary itself, though, further destroys the facility to articulate anything other than that which is innocent. Identity in relation to sexual violence is either victim or survivor, and both are assessed for innocence. Within practice Lyra is concerned that the vocabulary of sexual violence in particular is experienced as violent, as causing harm. Breaking the silence is both perceived of as personally re-traumatising and productive of others' vicarious trauma. So damaging are descriptions of sexual violence that trigger warnings are required. Unlike women who have experienced sexual violence, the reluctant hearer can choose not to listen in order to stave off any potential damage. Following Zizek's argument, though, the construction of such accounts as violent speech further delimits the articulation of abuse. To focus on the subjective violence of such descriptions is in actuality a smokescreen obscuring the underlying violence of categorisation.

Secondly, further consideration of the violence of categorisation is required as oppositional identities legitimise specific socially sanctioned behaviour and erase that which does not conform. Butler (2006) explains that the parameters of cultural intelligibility, the process by which a subject is recognisable as capable of living a life that counts, are reiterated within restraints of the (heteronormative) discursive matrix. Cultural intelligibility relies on counter processes of erasure which occur through abjection, or discursive omission. That is, discourse dehumanises or derealises in its failure to name. Oppression, therefore, operates not just through explicit prohibition but also covertly, exerting a normative violence through abjection, that which is rendered unthinkable and unnameable. Since such bodies do not figure in reality, it is impossible to register violence against the abject. In relation to sexual violence, then, cultural intelligibility is facilitated within the limits of the moral framework of victim-survivor duality. Albeit problematic, violence exerted against women who identify as victim-survivor is recognisable because they are named and defined within these categorisations. However, erased are experiences that lie outside the confines of victim-survivor identity, that are not recognised as 'innocent', and where definitions are rejected.

Fundamental to the affirmation and elimination of the subject is Butler's concept of recognition, a process emphasising the self as always in relation with others, and which marks the site of both intelligibility

DOI: 10.1057/9781137461728.0003

(or abjection) and of ethical practice. In naming and defining, recognition calls into existence a particular and viable subjectivity. Drawing on Hegel's notion of ek-stasis, the moment of standing outside of oneself during a rage or in a passion, Butler (2006: 4) argues that the self, experienced as others perceive it, is invited problematically into categorisation:

> I may feel that without some recognisability I cannot live. But I may also feel that the terms by which I am recognised make life unliveable. This is the juncture from which critique emerges, where critique is understood as an interrogation of the terms by which life is contained in order to open up the possibility of different modes of living.

Recognition is important to Butler because categories such as victim-survivor allow the possibility of a liveable life, but definitional constraints conversely make life unliveable. It is also the point at which an ethical relation is established. Exposed in ek-stasis is our vulnerability in connections with others. For example, Butler (2006: 22) suggests that loss is a form of dispossession and in grief and mourning 'something about who we are is revealed, something that delineates the ties we have to others, that shows us that these ties constitute who we are, ties or bonds that compose us'. The subject's susceptibility to the other is the basis of its vulnerability and also its ethical responsibilities. The prospect of violation and the need for attachment and dependency prompts an ethical response. However, for the abject, who are not hailed into actuality, there is no recognition at all. They remain under the radar, unrecognised and illegitimate.

Thirdly, given the significance of intersubjectivity and recognisability, how ethical a response is feminist practice that, in its assumption of the primacy of the survivor identity, compartmentalises experience. 'Survivor' functions as a regulatory ideal (Worrell 2003) that demands borders are policed and symbolically reproduces victim categorisation. Women's behaviour is judged and their experiences pitted against each other. Compartmentalisation is also evidenced in the conceptualisation of rape as non-violent. For women who encounter violence it is understood only as accidental (Lyra 2014), as different from the usual experience of rape, rather than illustrative of the colonising intent of all perpetrators. And for Lyra, practice that emphasises the expertise and resilience of certain professionals operating within the confines of the therapy room encloses male violence within confidentiality clauses

DOI: 10.1057/9781137461728.0003

and places perpetrators out of the reach of retribution or responsibility, thereby separating the 'private' experience of rape from public and political debate. This is not to suggest that feminist-based praxis and competence is irrelevant. Feminism is vital to question, rather than contribute to, the assessment and grading of women speaking from experience. Required is an ethical feminist praxis that is both critical of categorisation and embraces vulnerability. Otherwise any thorough analysis of violence per se is obfuscated and sexual violence is contained within boundaries that determine how it is experienced, and to whom, what, where, when, and how it can be communicated.

Conclusion

The embodied reality of sexually violent events is subsumed, predominantly through the language of psy-sciences, into a damaged and stigmatised identity. The contemporary representation of 'rape victim', an inherently vulnerable and careless woman, is so morally discreditable and tainted, that immediate transformation is required (Mardorossian 2014). However, in accounts from women who have experienced sexual violence there is evidence of an ambivalence in their negotiation of this particular subject position. Whilst the devastation of sexual violence necessarily impacts on her self-perception and her relations with others, any imposition of categorisation is frustrated. Moreover, in the articulation of shame and the operation of oppression, an alternative consideration of subjectivity is detailed. Rather than pursue identity as fixed, rational, and developmental, where rape is forced upon an already formed self, accounts suggest the complicit and resistive subject emerges in relation with others and within social structures, language, power, and moral codes. Furthermore, an indestructible human interrelation that always involves the possibility of the other renders impossible absolute dehumanisation. This theorisation of the self has three significant implications explored further in the following chapters.

Firstly, categorisation symbolically and actually delimits the life of women designated credible victims of rape as well as those who are not judged believable. To be recognised and called into the 'rape victim' identity position suggests a visibility that demands monitoring and evaluation, leaving the path to credibility narrow and treacherous for women whose experiences have become noticed. However, this

DOI: 10.1057/9781137461728.0003

identity positioning also relies upon unrecognisable and abject subjectivity. Of concern then is the sexually violated women who remain invisible and unnamed. Secondly, this theorisation of the self incorporates an articulation of female agency that is both complicit and resistive. It is suggested here that agency is not the female appropriation of male sexual assertiveness albeit limited in its expression for women by social constraints. Nor is it defined as different for women, so that personal acts of resistance and moments of passivity are re-evaluated in terms of agency (Mardorossian 2014). Rather, to avoid naturalising its association with masculinity, agency is an ethical self-transformation that challenges the boundaries of knowledge and truth but remains contained within the permissible. And thirdly, subjectivity constituted in dependence and vulnerability demands an ethical response. Although over time feminism has been superseded by psychology, diluted by funding cuts and financial restrictions, and publicly judged obsolete, in practice feminism offers an alternative and persuasive response to sexual violence, a political praxis rooted in self-determination that acknowledges vulnerability and accommodates varied experiences.

DOI: 10.1057/9781137461728.0003

3
Credibility

Abstract: *Chapter 3 focuses on credibility assessment as a mechanism of categorisation. In the psychological discourse of harm (O'Dell 2003) the 'rape victim' is articulated therapeutically as inevitably and enduringly damaged and stigmatised. So prolific is this discourse that it has become the measure of women's credibility and therefore their claim to truth. Within women's accounts a 'credibility conundrum' (Jordan 2004b) is identified that presents clearly the heavily policed and often impossible path to credibility, limited by the harm story. However, standing on the metaphorical cliff edge of disclosure, opportunities arise in strategies such as silence and avoidance to circumvent the inevitability of victimhood.*

Healicon, Alison. *The Politics of Sexual Violence: Rape, Identity and Feminism.* Basingstoke: Palgrave Macmillan, 2015. DOI: 10.1057/9781137461728.0004.

DOI: 10.1057/9781137461728.0004

I've got this thing about lying and my integrity and it was all to do with me and people's opinion of me, feeling unworthy, feeling I couldn't do me job, feeling dirty, feeling misunderstood.

I have this fear of not being believed.

(Eliza)

The fear of not being believed, of being cast a liar, is significant enough to silence women who have experienced rape and/or childhood sexual abuse and inhibits attempts at seeking advice, support, and justice. Women who have experienced sexual violence position themselves in relation to rape myths and victim blaming ideology, to both question the severity and reality of their experiences, and to assess how they are presenting themselves to others. Each encounter with family members, friends, and the wider community is problematic and risky as it contains cultural presumptions and judgements confirming the self-blame and shame she may already feel. Being believed, which is integral to personal integrity and identity, and derivative of shame, self-worth, and blame, is negotiated subjectively, in relationships with others, and within contextually specific and often contradictory discourses and is inextricably linked with credibility. Whether she is believed or not is felt to indicate something about who she is as a human being, an articulation of the value of her essential character. It is this evaluation of her personhood, the assessment of her credibility, that is prioritised over scrutiny of incidents of abuse and the role of the perpetrator in them. If deemed credible and therefore believable, then sexual violence took place and she is legitimated as a victim of abuse. If not, then she is castigated as a liar. Either way, the implications for her sense of self are significant.

This chapter considers some of the different ways in which credibility or incredibility is signified and assessed to understand the processes of categorisation and consequences for individual identity. Particularly focusing on feminist involvement in the 'harm story' (O'Dell 2003), a narrative that suggests sexual violence always causes psychological damage, this chapter considers the cost to the individual that victim plausibility is measured in terms of an appropriate expression of inevitable harm. The harm and trauma discourse as appropriated by feminist praxis is outlined first to suggest that the identity of the sexually violated woman is narrowly defined and actively exclusive. Then in order to

DOI: 10.1057/9781137461728.0004

consider nuance and contradictions to counter the inevitability of harm within this discourse, accounts from women interviewed which focus on the continual navigation of credibility are evaluated. This process to, and negotiation of, credibility suggests that within the discourse of harm and trauma, certain experiences are sensationalised, rendering those with different experiences deceitful. But for those few whose experiences are accepted as credible, as a category, the legitimate victim is also problematic.

The story of trauma and harm

Inherent within the story of trauma and harm (O'Dell 2003), a particularly prolific psychological discourse, is the notion of inevitable and long-term emotional damage caused by the physical, sexual, and psychological corruption of an innocent child or child-like victim (Reavey and Warner 2003). In its appropriation of the scientific language of neurobiology, this story suggests that childhood sexual abuse devastates the hard wiring in the brain, not only causing psychological problems but also definitively interrupting the psychological maturation of the child. As such she is always different from, and deficient to, her 'normally' developing counterpart (Burman 2003). Although adult women may not have their sense of self stunted, but fragmented, their experiences are similarly couched in psychological language of stress, dissociative and personality disorders, trauma, and damage. So totalising is this discourse that any absence of trauma response is attributed to denial, implying an eventual incapacitation as trauma manifests itself unexpectedly. The medicalisation and pathologisation of the effects of sexual violence and the sexually violated individual within this discourse necessitates specialist psychological and sustained intervention. Prominent therapists such as Batmanghelidjh (2006) and Rothschild (2000) suggest that in order to reconnect the synaptic breakages, the individual requires not only long-term psychological and therapeutic support but also on-going care with which active engagement is imperative. For it is in the acknowledgement and verbalisation of abuse within therapy that the individual actively participates in her own recovery to manage symptoms and process trauma.

The harm story is encapsulated and politicised within the feminism of Herman's (2001) book *Trauma and Recovery*, which is renowned within the field of sexual violence. Herman incorporates the experiences of

DOI: 10.1057/9781137461728.0004

sexually violated women into an analysis of the psychological damage sustained in terror and manifested in symptoms of trauma to situate her diagnosis of 'complex post-traumatic stress disorder' within the social context. In the detail of the effects of trauma, as an expression of a legitimate response to oppression and the misuse of male power, the severity and impact of abuse is undeniable. Once diagnosed, Herman (2001: 1) proposes a staged approach to recovery that involves '(r)emembering and telling the truth about terrible events'. The political act of processing trauma through speaking out facilitates the possibility of personal and social transformation. Although trauma and shame render problematic attempts at remembering, within the safety of the therapeutic environment, incoherent memories can be analysed to regain control stolen in rape and trauma. This engagement with therapy is not only significant for the recovery of the individual but, in detailing the truth contained in memory, the social conditions in which sexual violence is tolerated are exposed. In naming and detailing the experience of the trauma of oppression, Herman (2001: 209) suggests a 'victim's' 'life story is a gift to others'.

There is no doubt that the feminist appropriation of the harm story provides a common language with which to describe and make sense of the devastating impact of abuse. It offers a coherent explanation, substantiated through science, to counter disbelief and justify previously misunderstood reactions to sexual violence. For example, Siegel's (1999) 'Window of Tolerance' model, employed in some feminist therapeutic practice to enable women to integrate tolerable rather than traumatic experiences, legitimises the necessity of flight and freeze reactions. That is, there are physiological responses to traumatic events that challenge the idea that women should fight back. Feminist reformulation of the discourse of harm offers a framework for psychological interventions and strategies for healing and provides an ethos linking individual experiences to wider social practices. In voicing these culturally marginalised experiences within the confines of the therapeutic situation, she asserts her agency and takes control of her recovery, and accurately representing the social context necessarily challenges misogyny within institutions that support male violence.

However, Herman's prescriptive and therapeutic approach relies on, and sustains, a categorisation of trauma that alludes to, rather than thoroughly engages with, concepts of truth, memory, and transformation. Indeed, Herman's exposition of trauma is indicative of a feminist

DOI: 10.1057/9781137461728.0004

involvement in the trauma story that paradoxically reified medical categorisation (O'Dell 2003) and operates to constrain women's behaviour because it frames the criteria on which credibility is assessed. This discourse presumes the necessity of a prescribed and therapeutic recovery, defined in the move away from victimhood as an identity position to that of survivor, further compartmentalising and categorising experiences of rape. Utilising safety as justification, this discourse confines the articulation of sexual violence to the therapeutic relationship that is managed by experts and bounded by confidentiality. In the following sections, truth, memory, and transformation as critical concepts are problematised and considered from the viewpoint of women's accounts because they are implicated in processes to credibility. Feminism has campaigned systematically to have all sexual violence acknowledged independently of credibility criteria, and yet within this discourse certain women and certain types of sexual violence are seen as more credible than others, and it limits what women say and do. In buying into a specific discourse, it is argued here that complexity and contradictions cannot be easily accommodated and so experience outside of the credible is left not only unexplained but to have experiences rendered incredible is particularly painful.

Telling the truth

It is in the judicial system that ascertaining and extricating the truth from an individual is procedurally necessary. Having credibility, signified in an inherent believability and truthfulness, involves complex cultural criteria not only about the incident(s) of sexual violence, but also around the innocence and culpability of 'victims' that is particularly apparent within, but not exclusive to, encounters in criminal justice systems. As research on attrition in the UK (Kelly et al. 2005; Myhill and Allen 2002) and on attitudes to rape complainants in New Zealand (Jordan 2004a; 2004b) suggests, certain experiences of sexual violence are assessed as more serious and therefore more genuine than others based on their proximity to 'real rape' (Estrich 1987). The further away the experience was from physically violent and evidential stranger rape, the less credibility the incident of sexual violence was perceived to have. Indeed women often trivialise their experiences in comparison with 'real rape' criteria and so exclude themselves from the reporting process. Even

DOI: 10.1057/9781137461728.0004

though these studies argue that proportionally stranger rape is relatively rare in comparison to sexual violence by someone known to the victim, the truth about sexual violence is located in 'real rape', the criterion with which others are judged and inevitably found unbelievable and incredible.

However, the truth of sexual violence and therefore the credibility of the sexually violated woman are not only situated in 'real rape' criteria. There are also categories of women who report their experiences of sexual violence to the police and are deemed less credible and indeed incredible. For example, these studies found that women who were in a relationship with the perpetrator, or who had been drinking, were prostituted, had mental ill health, were learning disabled, and/or had previously reported experiences of sexual violence (i.e., had been re-victimised), were likely to have their cases 'no further action-ed'. Whether a reported rape is pursued in the criminal justice system continues to rely on the assessment of the individual 'victim's' morality and credibility. Such police practice assumes that being drunk or prostituted are symptomatic of an irresponsible and questionable character, whilst women who have mental ill health, are learning disabled, or are re-victimised are unable to articulate what happened or confused because of their 'limited' mental capacities. Women who have had a sexual relationship with the perpetrator are similarly culpable because their character rendered them incapable of exiting the relationship sooner.

Moreover, a recent report (Coffey 2014) suggests such credibility criteria that attribute sexual violence to the deficiencies in women are utilised in assessing children's entitlement to support or justice. Evaluating the scale of child sexual exploitation in Greater Manchester, Coffey highlights major concerns with organisational decisions. For example, Coffey (2014: 98) suggests, the language used to justify

> cases unfit for further action by the CPS,… included the fact that the girl wore cropped tops. 'The victim is known (as highlighted by social workers) to tend to wear sexualised clothes when she is out of school, such as cropped tops.'

> In one case the file read: 'Because of her record and her unsettled background… she is far from an ideal victim.' In another: 'I note her father has referred to her to a social worker as being a slag, saying she is responsible for what has happened.'

Criteria to assess her believability and credibility, to identify the 'ideal victim', therefore involve attempts to ascertain her innocence, morality,

DOI: 10.1057/9781137461728.0004

and ability to produce a coherent account of the event(s). It is argued here that this assessment is not restricted to the criminal justice process, or to adult women, as the harm story also exacerbates, rather than eradicates, the assessment of credibility.

This body of research has documented the systematic exclusion of certain experiences of sexual violence and certain categories of women by the police, and Jordan (2004b) suggests that pervasive beliefs about women as intrinsically deceitful colour practices that actively undermine the credibility of the complainant. Specifically Jordan (2004b) identifies a 'credibility conundrum' where police doubt a woman when she alleges rape but believe her retraction. Within the trauma and harm story truth is a fundamental construct on which the credibility of the individual is assessed because telling the truth opens the door to support, justice, and recovery. So, here a similar credibility conundrum emerges. If a woman appears unhurt by her experiences of sexual violence, then she is not believed. Her credibility is questioned as it is assumed she would be seriously and visibly affected. However, if a woman is consumed by trauma and unable to maintain any control over trauma symptoms, she is also rendered incredible as she becomes pathologised, psychiatrically labelled, or, if perceived as beyond treatment, abandoned by the medical establishment.

Ultimately Jordan (2004b) argues that within the constabulary there is a presumption that women lie when they report rape. That is, credibility is based on assumptions which suggest a woman's essential disposition is questionable, that it is in her very nature to lie. Her character is both deficient and deceitful, and this is apparent in accounts from women interviewed about their encounters with others outside of the criminal justice system. In these excerpts, the process by which truth is negotiated is demonstrably complex, and they suggest that credibility is rarely approved and difficult to secure. The consequences are that telling becomes too difficult but both identity positions, victim and liar, are equally resisted. The following excerpts focus on the moment of disclosure and contain meaning in excess of the point argued here. However, they are chosen to suggest that in these moments of telling credibility is called into question and simultaneously a space is created in which the dilemma of being victim or liar is negotiated, accepted, or refuted.

> (On telling her first psychologist) I think they were just gobsmacked at first, I think it was just unbelievable because they couldn't believe what I'd been through. And it took them a while to get it out of me. (Amy)

DOI: 10.1057/9781137461728.0004

The act of telling someone... was weird and always the hardest part but it was like a real catharsis, kind of thing. I didn't tell anybody for years what had happened to me and I was totally in denial, like basically it's not worth commenting on, it's not worth telling anybody... although I really hated telling people I started to tell different close friends, people I hadn't told before, because it was a way of... acknowledging that something had happened and feeling that you are not just going mad. You know it sounds almost a bit indulgent but you'd get that attention off somebody and that sympathy for that period of time you get that intense shock and sympathy and you think 'oh alright, it is a thing, I'm allowed to feel', you know?... You minimise it so much yourself, you kind of want somebody to take the responsibility away from you of having to acknowledge it, 'oh well if they think it's bad I'm allowed to feel like it is.' (Ruby)

I actually don't think I realised until I said the words... how I felt. I honestly don't remember feeling it at all until the night I told her (friend) and I can remember it so clearly and the second I said it, it just flooded, this realisation that what I was saying was real because I remember thinking in my head, as I was telling her the words, I had a voice in my head saying 'you're lying, you're lying, this isn't true' but I knew it was true and you know she was really upset. But it's been really weird, I've only ever managed to tell people, say if I was staying at a friend's and certain situations, you know I wouldn't be able to just tell them if we went for a drink, you know it's strange. (Ruby)

I went to university when I was 19 and I was in my second year and I had a breakdown completely out of the blue and I found myself wandering around not knowing why I was there or what I was doing. Friends would say that I would sit rocking and staring into space and at the time I put it down to stress. You know I was working really hard. And a lot of students do a lot of very odd things and so on. And I was desperately ashamed of going from super-competent to super-incompetent and that re-evaluation of myself, I did what I could to get out of that. And I had some memories at the time of abuse that kind of came out of nowhere and that I really thought I was making up. I remember watching myself tell my tutor that my granddad had abused me and thinking 'why are you saying that?' It's like 'you liar!' (laughs). Really that sense of being out of body, watching yourself say it and thinking 'you are in so much trouble now for making that stuff up. Such an evil thing to do.' But evidently somebody, I was watching another part of me, me, asking for help really. And I sort of pushed it all down again and carried on. (Caitlin)

These excerpts identify the point of disclosure as a convergence of the harm discourse, and an internalised struggle with truth and credibility

DOI: 10.1057/9781137461728.0004

in the process of recognition and identification. Within the trauma and harm discourse the sexually violated woman is subjected to bodily leakages and impulses, which compel her to reveal a truth hidden not only from others but also from herself. The revelation of truth as it escapes in flashback, nightmares, body memories, and then through the spontaneous articulation of experience, is evidence of the impact of abuse as described in the harm story. But its significance isn't fully recognised as it is assessed in accordance with stereotypical credibility criteria of 'real rape' and their understanding of their personal deficiencies. The risk involved in disclosure is that the sexually violated woman metaphorically stands on a precipice where her identity is potentially transformed into either innocent victim or liar. Although victimhood would facilitate the absolution of responsibility and their legitimate claim to the pain of abuse, women in these interviews acknowledge their deficiencies, whether that is being unbelievable, unworthy, or incompetent. So since victimhood is ascribed only to innocents, those with no deficiencies and with experiences that correspond with 'real rape', the only alternative is to be a liar, to have made it up.

If as Jordan (2004b) suggests it is assumed that all women have an essential propensity to lie, then innocence as truth, the main component for assessing credibility, is inevitably unobtainable. In the harm story innocence remains present in the psychologically damaged child victim, different from her 'normally' developing counterpart and forever defined in relation to her experiences of sexual abuse (Burman 2003). Woodiwiss (2009: 19) explores this 'status of innocence' to suggest that it relies on a particular narrative of abuse which renders victims entirely passive and where acts of resistance are omitted. As such, Woodiwiss (2009: 20) suggests that 'passive acquiescence is the circulating narrative framework necessary for the victim to avoid blame'. Entitlement to the status of innocence excludes the sexually violated adult woman by virtue of her deficient character and essential deceitfulness and is denied to those individuals who either exchange favours for abuse or exercise any control. Even children, deemed complicit in this way, have their status rescinded, and all are then subject to blame. For example, Coffey's (2014) report suggests that in the 2013 review of child sexual exploitation in Rochdale, the children involved were defined as child prostitutes, the sexual abuse they experienced was therefore determined as self-inflicted, and so due to their perceived lack of innocence, they were excluded from victim status. In denial and postponing engagement with trauma, these

DOI: 10.1057/9781137461728.0004

excerpts indicate that women here are reluctant to be defined in relation to such limiting yet pervasive categorisation and so stave off blame, even if it is only temporarily.

Disclosure signifies a moment in identity positioning where the discourse of harm converges with victim blaming mythology located in gendered assumptions about the deceitfulness and character deficiencies of women. The inevitability of harm renders possible only an identity position that involves negotiating perpetual difference and continual assessment of credibility because the main criteria, innocence and truth, are out of reach. Furthermore, these accounts demonstrate that the jump into the abyss of continual credibility assessment is not inevitable, and disclosure offers a space where innocence and deceitfulness can be avoided.

Memory, truth, and credibility

It has been argued so far that disclosure threatens an individual's identity as it marks the beginning of her participation in a process of continual assessment of her credibility. On disclosing abuse she measures herself and gauges her behaviour, and is assessed by others, in the social production of the sexually violated woman as defined in the harm story and victim blaming mythology. In the following accounts truth and credibility are further compounded because of the unpredictability and unreliability of memory. Given that credibility is evaluated in terms of a coherent presentation of an essential truth, women interviewed were acutely aware of the limits to, and gaps in, their memory of significant events. Memory was discussed as slippery and confusing and not entirely trustworthy but, simultaneously, revealed an embodied and sometimes elusive truth. The trauma and harm discourse valorises the problems of unreliable and fragmented memories because they testify to the distress caused in the traumatic event. However, these accounts demonstrate that in order to get to the truth hidden in trauma, and to secure recovery, ultimately, memory required deciphering through the storying of the event. Again, these excerpts are profound in their scope and only an element of meaning is utilised.

> With me it started at the age of 5 with me dad molesting me. Me mum was beating me black and blue with a belt that I have no memory of but it's in my file. (Amy)

But then I come up with memories. It's really difficult because it's like where have I got this memory from? Why suddenly have I got this memory? ... It was terrible because I just felt it was another abuse that I had not come to terms with. And it's like ... how many more are going to pop into my head and how many more people have been at me that I don't remember because I have been through too much. (Amy)

Victoria: I feel like the memories are here, for example, I am walking around the shop and suddenly I see the picture of when I was six and I see this house or that forest ... I feel I am walking there and then I try to grab it and it goes .... It's a strange desire to want to know the truth, to get rid of the mould from my mind. I want to feel it but I can imagine it to be horrible.

Alison: So it's something about knowing the truth then

Victoria: Feeling it and knowing it. I remember something, all these flash-backs, all these strange feelings but I don't know how to get there. I don't know how to get to that moment, how many times it happened, because sometimes it's one, two, or three times and the places I remember and I want to get at it.

I was tortured with electric shocks and things like that and I would feel that in my body, that acid feeling suddenly in my veins, so, so often, and that was particularly connected to the injunction not to tell anybody, and so whenever I told somebody part of my story, I mean for a couple of years it was nobody apart from (my husband) and my therapist, and then in another situation I told somebody, the first time I'd ever told somebody outside of that group, and that night I was up all night in absolute agony with this torture pain flooding through me that triggered it again, but I didn't have the memories of that properly then, and that started that narrative flowing. Those memories have come out, I verbalised them, put them into a kind of historical context, and amazingly the physical pain has lessened. It is amazing and such a relief. (Caitlin)

In terms of the amnesia of having a baby (as a result of ritual abuse) when I was 12 years old, I had a narrative of myself with the doctors and nurses and people generally that I had not ever had a baby. And then when you recall that you have had a baby, that is weird when you sit with the doctor and the doctor says, for a coil fitting or something like that, 'oh your notes say you haven't had a baby' and you say 'well I kind of have', and they're looking at you 'well either you have or you haven't, which is it?' and you think, well I've got memories of having had, but I didn't used to have memories of it and it's not been on my medical records and there's that whole uncertainty, and you think 'well have I or haven't I?' Everything from the symptoms and the flashbacks and the memories and all your alters telling you ... you definitely had a baby and yet your medical notes don't say you had a baby, you know? (Caitlin)

DOI: 10.1057/9781137461728.0004

The validity of the notion of recovered memory, as a mechanism to elucidate a credible truth, is theoretically and practically contentious. The harm story relies on a theorisation that suggests extreme trauma severs the link between memory of the event and the event itself yet truth is recoverable through careful therapeutic interpretation of escaped fragments of memory that are triggered over a number of years. Credibility, and therefore truth, in these fragmented accounts, are located in the understanding that trauma produces a profound and devastating effect on memory. However, the credibility of recovered memories as the exposition of truth, so central to the harm story, was seriously undermined with the introduction of False Memory Syndrome (Haaken 1998). A politically motivated movement championing False Memory Syndrome suggested it was induced through inappropriate therapeutic practice that would infer from vague memories experiences of abuse that could never be clearly articulated nor corroborated. As such, False Memory Syndrome overwhelmingly impacted on personal and collective experiences of abuse because it reasserted the application of the 'storehouse' model of memory (Campbell 2010) which relies on the articulation of an incontrovertible and objective truth directly linked in memory and not compromised over time or by over-enthusiastic therapists. As the personal accounts above testify, the need to know the truth is frustrated by the effects of trauma, but women question their own credibility as there is no definitive link to abusive events decipherable in fragments of their memory. In terms of collective understanding, the storehouse model rendered incredible ritual and cultic abuse because their identification and distinctiveness depended upon the presence of participants' recovered memory (Scott 2001).

Although the harm story provided an explanation to justify the credibility of incomplete and recovered memory, a critique to decentralise memory as the significant condition of trauma developed in opposition to both the storehouse model and the harm story. In order to avoid silencing women whose experiences of sexual abuse are incoherent and irretrievable, distanced from 'real rape' or too incredible and unbelievable, an alternative consideration of memory has been proffered that questions the link between memory and credibility. This proposition suggests that memory is both a cultural and contextual (re)production and like identity, which involves an active and on-going process that changes depending on current understandings and concerns. That is memories 'do not have to be fixed and singular in meaning in order to bear witness

DOI: 10.1057/9781137461728.0004

to the reality of the past' (Campbell 2010: 184). This is important because Warner (2007: 65) would argue that 'rather than trying to find out "what really happened" [a process which relies on recovering memories] people need to know that there are good reasons why their memories may be incomplete'. Given that sexual violence is discursively defined in psychological terms, and has implications for how women come to know themselves, telling can be dangerous, not only bodily, through the labelling of psychiatric conditions requiring surveillance and medication (Warner and Wilkins 2003; Proctor 2007), but also in relation to identity as it is defined in memory. Warner (2007) therefore calls into question directly the centrality of memory and instead acknowledges power relations within which stories of abuse are told.

In the above accounts elusive, partial, and bodily memories were recognised as troubling the traditional storehouse model of memory as fixed and connected to truth and suggest an appropriation of the harm story's prominence of recovered memory as evidence of credibility. However, these excerpts also reveal the necessity of a critique that not only questions essential truths and fixed memory but severs truth from credibility and situates experience within specific cultural contexts and power dynamics that prioritise and legitimate only certain stories and particular experiences.

Credibility in transformation

Herman (2001) acknowledges power dynamics, especially those sustaining patriarchy, and suggests gendered inequality can be challenged through an active personal and political engagement with the trauma implicit in all experiences of sexual violence. Her starting point is the acknowledgement of the severity of rape. However, in order to further elucidate the 'credibility conundrum' that suggests participation in recovery is constrained by assumptions that trauma is necessarily and permanently damaging but necessitates the management of the signs of trauma, this section focuses on three particular elements in the process to self-transformation. In disclosure, the individual is required to embark on a specific journey that involves the articulation of trauma and acceptance of harm, both of which have significant implications to self-perception. Deviation from this prescribed pathway is curtailed through assessment and is connected to credibility. It is argued here firstly that women experience assessment of credibility as a judgement on their character and as such implicates their access to support. Secondly, negotiation of the criteria of continual assessment involves anticipation of, and engagement with, cultural expectations about the impact of sexual violence and in which only certain responses are validated. Thirdly, moments of resistance absent from the prescription of the harm story are highlighted. Just as Herman (2001) argues, acknowledging the severity of rape is required, but accounts from women detail the nuances of the daily negotiation on the path to credibility that suggest a more ambivalent relationship with recovery as a prescription for transformation.

The following excerpts were chosen because they clearly articulate how individuals assess their own credibility in relation to character and support Jordan's (2004b) assertion that women speak from a position of having to challenge the assumption that they are lying. Credibility matters, but also apparent here is that it is located in the deficiencies of women.

I never used to blame myself for being prostituted until I started to talk about some things. Trying to heal hurt me a lot because I never stopped getting told 'you chose it', 'you still did it'. Compassion goes out the window as soon as people hear money is involved. Though I didn't even want or need money. HE did (the pimp). And in a million years I never chose it and 'I' didn't do it ... I was brainwashed using thought reform. Broken. There are so many 'helplines' I can't talk to now. They always end up blaming me .... However, I can talk about how I blamed myself for incest as a child. After all, everyone tells you it's not your fault. And these days no-one blames me for knocking on his door when I was a child or for the fact that he made me orgasm. They understand about children having to live in the situation they can't get out of. But people don't even understand that pimps control women and girls ... they don't understand that women cannot get away from the pimps, and how the pimps, men, and society sell and buy women and girls. They don't understand how soul destroying it is to be bought and sold and used and thrown away. (Maya)

(As a young women Donna and her friend were entrapped by a man they barely knew, in an isolated house in the French countryside.) It was absolutely terrifying ... I couldn't see a way out of it. She wasn't going to do it. I think because when I was 15 my boyfriend raped me, so I think, looking back at it now, I think I said 'I'll go sleep with him.' It was ok for me to do that because it happened to me before, so I was protecting her because she had not been damaged, if you like. I'd been damaged once so it was ok. One of us had to do it so I said 'right' and went in. So I was complicit, see

DOI: 10.1057/9781137461728.0004

I'm shaking now, I was absolutely terrified for my life and he, he did the dirty deed I don't know how many times that night. And I just lay there and I didn't resist but I didn't comply also. It was just, I just switched off completely. (Donna)

(In therapy) we've uncovered so many reasons why I consider myself as weak, partly physically weak cos it happened in the first place, psychologically weak cos I allowed it to happen. I'm starting to believe those things aren't true but it's not easy. And then there was the weakness of not doing something about it. (Dawn)

You get mixed up on what you've said. When I gave my statement (to the police) I kept thinking 'why did I say that because that couldn't have been, it couldn't have …' And I never thought they check your medical records and I got the date wrong of the termination…. And I couldn't sleep for another night then because I'm thinking I've lied…. Well it was integrity being questioned *(Alison: at every step)* At every step. Every step. Erm 'where was your lamp?' 'what did you have on?' 'Did you have knickers on?' 'well did he take them off?' … It never occurred to me that they would ask questions like that. (Eliza)

You see the difficulty with my situation is that I had slept with him before on one occasion I think. (Eliza)

(After she has made her statement with the policewoman) And I remember laughing with her but walking out feeling like I had no clothes on. (Eliza)

Each of these excerpts reveals a struggle with credibility defined through criterion of innocence already outlined by Jordan (2004a and b), Kelly et al. (2005), and Myhill and Allen (2002), and consequently in comparison, each woman finds herself lacking and incredible. Women who have experienced sexual violence often speak of there being something deficient about themselves that somehow invited, and continues to invite, abuse. For Maya innocence is operationally associated with children who are abused rather than afforded to herself as a formerly prostituted woman. Although she contends that her previous experiences of childhood sexual abuse have been culturally legitimated through acceptance that children have no power or choice in abusive situations, the personal deficiencies which have made her incredible and therefore ineligible for support are centred on her re-victimisation, prostitution, and involvement in cultic abuse. Donna also re-victimised is rendered incredible because of her previous experience of rape that she says damaged her. Although she didn't fight, as is socially expected of victims of rape (perhaps experienced as another deficiency), she feels she didn't comply

DOI: 10.1057/9781137461728.0004

either but instead avoided the corruption of her innocent friend who she felt was so different from her own polluted self. Dawn felt herself to be wholly weak and Eliza, whose deficiency lies in her having chosen as a sexual partner the man who raped her, expresses for all, the overwhelming sense of shame.

In each of these excerpts women suggest their character was so deficient it not only set them apart from non-abused women but was also implicit in assessment of their lack of credibility. Although for Jordan (2004b) assessing truth or lies was specific to police investigations, these accounts suggest the negotiation of credibility is encountered much more widely: indeed credibility permeates all social encounters. Whether credibility is approved or not, and given that innocence is rarely assigned, having to participate in a continual process of assessment is keenly felt. Women here recognised that they would be judged deficient because they saw their own 'deficiencies' clearly, and this was merely confirmed in their encounters with others. This is of significance if, as the trauma story suggests, recovery contributes to credibility. As suggested in these excerpts, women already judge themselves in relation to victim blaming mythology often prohibiting themselves from accessing support. Women also anticipate such responses in all encounters, and depending on the assessment of credibility required in support and justice services, they may be excluded, which in turn further reduces their credibility.

It seems clear here that the preponderance and proliferation of cultural myths which justify victim blaming in situations of sexual violence is hard to escape, especially when each encounter involves an assessment of her essential character in order to ascertain truth or lies. This can dictate whether or not she is entitled to support and opportunities for justice. Complicit in the predominance of victim blaming mythology is the trauma story where the expression of harm is a measure of credibility and truth but where credibility is approved only within specific culturally sanctioned parameters of legitimate behaviour. Her credibility, the 'truth' about the assault(s), and therefore the seriousness with which abuse is taken, is measured in relation to the depth and length of behaviour accepted as denoting trauma. Thus, in the trauma story, although sexual violence is inevitably traumatic and devastating, the responsible victim has to be seen to access appropriate support in order to secure her own recovery; otherwise, and argued here, she is positioned outside of credibility. Warner (2003) proffers the notion of the 'recovered woman' which relies on an illusion that confessing to or disclosing abuse leads

DOI: 10.1057/9781137461728.0004

to greater self-knowledge when it actually brings more efficient regulation and normalisation through self-policing subjects. Recovery in these instances focuses on the individual and obscures interaction in each social encounter. Warner (2003: 231) says,

> The fictive separation between personal and social serves to concretise 'recovered' women as self-disciplining subjects set in opposition to 'unrecovered' women – who are out there, dangerous and unpredictable. The recovered woman is 'open about her problems' and has 'insight'. This woman is no longer 'out of control'.

Credibility therefore is more likely to be assigned if she expresses an 'appropriate' amount of controllable harm because she has accessed and is engaging with suitable support.

On the other hand, in her concern to question victimhood as an inevitable consequence of sexual violence, Lamb (1999) highlights the moral judgements that exist for women who feel 'no repercussions' from sexual violence. She argues that contemporary cultural assumptions dictate that only in situations where the incident(s) were actively trivialised or deemed not to have taken place is it accepted that sexual violence is not traumatising. That is, rape is considered inevitably traumatising and therefore women who are unaffected by their experiences are judged as liars; their experiences are not believed and are discredited. All in all, it is a tricky and narrowly defined path trod by women who have experienced sexual violence and one that necessitates a particular performance that accedes to trauma but is manageable. To be either out of control and unrecovered or to be unaffected leads to a loss of credibility; women are not believed and are excluded from further or any support or justice. This proscriptive and limiting performance required of the sexually violated woman in an on-going process to credibility is articulated clearly by Eliza:

> I remember a woman who worked in a (chemist), in a big town, Manchester, Liverpool, I can't remember and she was raped by the pharmacist ... and it went to Crown Court and I think he got off because what they were saying 'how could she go back to work straight after that'. And I knew why she did because why the bloody hell shouldn't she? Why shouldn't she, she's done nothing wrong. It's an act of defiance that. That's not weakness. That's strength.
>
> Because of the job I do and I'm meeting police and I see CID and I had a CID officer who knew about my [story], because he actually said 'why

didn't you tell me' and then I saw him out when I was with my friends, one night after I'd reported it and I've never, ever, done that ever, (indicating a really low cut top) but that's ok but I just haven't and I had a blouse on and I kept thinking, I said to [my friend] 'can you see it?' (covering up her chest with her hands) 'does he think I'm a ...' and then I was dancing and I'm dancing and enjoying myself and I'm thinking 'oh no this isn't as it should be!' I should be at home rocking (curling herself up in a foetal position and rocking on her chair).

So totalising is the trauma story that an individual knows the parameters of appropriate behaviour because she feels the weight of social judgement and boundaries are policed. It seems that the sexually violated woman is expected not to cope with everyday life in the immediate aftermath and therefore an early return to work raises suspicions about the truth of her account. Similarly given that trauma is devastating, to be seen out enjoying herself also jeopardises her claim to credibility. But at the same time, as Warner (2003) suggests, she is also expected to access support and recover, so giving up work altogether indicates that she is uncontrolled, unmanaged, and also incredible. Eliza articulates the constant negotiation of identity on a prescribed path to credibility and in so doing troubles the staged approach to recovery which relies on indeterminable points in a delineated process. What is acceptable behaviour and where each stage begins and ends is variable yet is assumed and employed in judgement. Eliza also questions who decides credibility in order to pass through the gateway to support and justice. The assignment of credibility is so intangible that the need to conform to prescribed behaviour is not derived from the necessity to continue as credible (as she may not have been originally granted credibility), but rather to avoid jeopardising her credibility further.

It seems that whoever women are and whatever women do, their identity as a sexually violated woman is assessed and found lacking in relation to the trauma story and victim blaming mythology. However, although deviation from the process to credibility has serious and devastating implications for women, including being disregarded and excluded from services or medicated and psychiatrically labelled, the above accounts suggest there are resistances to such a totalising discourse. As proposed by women interviewed here, the identity of the sexually violated woman is questioned in order to avoid shame and credibility assessment. Gavey (1999; 2005) and Lockwood Harris (2011) have also considered resistance to rape victim identity. In order to avoid the psychological implications of

DOI: 10.1057/9781137461728.0004

being categorised as a rape victim Gavey (2005: 176) 'found only around 30–50% of women who affirm that they have had an experience which meets the narrow definition of rape identify that they have experienced something they call "rape"'. Whilst Lockwood Harris (2011) demonstrates that women avoided the term rape to describe their experience because it reduced the complexity of their relationship with the perpetrator, and with whom they had a relationship, to an act of violence and determined that they should leave. Both suggest that in their avoidance of the term rape, women are questioning the limited and limiting vocabulary which reduces complex relationships to essentialist and fixed categories that not only deny agency but determine a specific course of action.

Lockwood Harris (2011) employs the concept of 'grey rape' in instances where rape categorisation is both evaded and alluded to. 'Grey rape' is evident in the following accounts:

> I find it very hard to use the word 'rape' and hate it, I really hate it, and I used to say it but my friends would be like 'well you have been'...In my counselling...it was almost like Stockholm syndrome or something, having sort of sympathies for, not really for the two guys who were watching but for the other guy, thinking well, you know, maybe. I used to have this weird habit – I was obsessed with not being unfair to him, so I would say to (my counsellor), well I'm not going to call it rape, cos what if I'm wrong? She said well you don't even know that person so it doesn't matter, but I said...what if I'm saying something totally unfair to him and it's not even true? (Ruby)

> I also consider myself quite a liberal person...and I feel strongly about miscarriages of justice and people being branded for things they haven't done.... And so in our law course you learn about how a crime does not happen without intention, and to me rape is a crime, and if the guy who tried to have sex with me didn't realise or didn't mean to do it or didn't realise I didn't want to then, although (her counsellor) said it didn't make a difference, it did to me. (Ruby)

> I knew what had happened. And I just put all my make up on and went to work. I kinda questioned what had happened but I chose not to think that that's what happened because it's not what you see on films (laughs). This is the problem. Rape is when they hold you down, you scream, you break your nails, you know...you get the vase, you get the lamp and you beat them and you try and protect yourself. Then you stagger to the phone, you know, with a broken arm. You don't get up in the morning, put your make-up on, do you? That's not what you see on telly. (Eliza)

> It's going back to the same thing – what's rape? He just messed with a knife (indicating at her stomach) and threatened me with my kids, he didn't

DOI: 10.1057/9781137461728.0004

assault me, but what choice did I have cos, there was no choice to make at that time. You think you'd pick the phone up, don't you. You don't! You don't because you are too scared. You know that I know that, they don't know that out there, do they, because people don't understand. (Eliza)

Hesitation about defining experience as rape, suggested in these accounts, reveals a complicated situation. Both women question the truth of their experiences yet allude to the seriousness of them. Ruby was worried he may not have understood her refusal to consent – was it a misunderstanding? In not fighting her abuser and getting ready as usual for work Eliza similarly questions her experiences. Ruby and Eliza negotiate cultural assumptions which deny rape in situations where women are perceived to give mixed messages or are immediately unaffected by trauma. Moreover, Gavey and Schmidt (2011) suggest the trauma of rape discourse impacts on everyday understandings of sexual violence, which coalesce around rape as a special kind of trauma, unique and beyond everyday experience. Therefore, simultaneously, the trivialisation of sexual violence through the denial of certain experiences is offset against the sensationalisation of rape as a fate worse than death. Even though Ruby and Eliza's experiences were relatively close to the 'real rape' scenario, in their eyes there are sufficient discrepancies to cast doubt on their interpretation of it as rape. In their internalisation of society's unobtainable rape criteria, they assess their experiences as trivial. However, it could be argued, that 'grey rape', that which avoids defining experiences as rape as evidenced in these accounts, implies a resistance to the harm story and victim blaming mythology. Maybe it is not about trivialising, but rather avoiding the destruction of their identity that experiencing rape predictably involves and actively circumventing the inevitability of victimhood, including an engagement with a denial of agency, credibility criteria, and the delimiting process to recovery.

Conclusion

O'Dell (2003) situates the discourse of harm, which presupposes the inevitability of trauma and psychological damage, in the 1970s when psychology, in its pursuit of absolute scientific truth, established itself as the rightful authority to define and explain sexual violence. Not only was feminism as a politically alternative response to sexual violence sidelined, but elements of the trauma story were incorporated into existing feminist

DOI: 10.1057/9781137461728.0004

praxis. Whilst for some the proliferation of a therapeutic approach evidenced depoliticisation (Furedi 2004; Becker 2005), this discourse recognised the significance of sexual violence, legitimated women's psychological responses to adverse situations, and centred on agency and personal transformation. The story of harm provided tools and hope for women struggling with the trauma of abuse. However, although offering a more sympathetic understanding of the impact of sexual violence, Gavey and Schmidt (2011) suggest that, nevertheless, once categorised within a stigmatised identity the individual is more easily subjected to various forms of symbolic violence. Prioritising trauma above interrelations of power, the harm story has created further conditions with which to assess the 'rape victim's' credibility. Indeed, in its insistence on the inevitability of damage, the story of harm has become the measure of truth and credibility, defining women's experiences and confining the presentation and articulation of sexual violence.

The ideal rape victim, as a categorisation, is an inevitably contemporary identity position that requires incontrovertible truth, innocence, proportionate expression of trauma, and immediate dissociation, preferably through recovery. Framed in the discourse of harm, the perfect victim is an unobtainable and regulatory ideal operating within Zizek's (2009) 'fantasmatic dimension,' always present but out of reach, functioning as the standard by which women's credibility is assessed and truth verified. In its internalisation, the ideal victim becomes a self-defining and self-regulating archetype. Categorisation of the ideal rape victim operates in conjunction with processes of compartmentalisation, where certain experiences of rape are considered more 'real' or credible than others. Both rely on trivialisation and sensationalisation techniques that distort women's understanding of their embodied experience of sexual violence and trauma. Accounts from women facilitate a different analysis of living in the aftermath of sexual violence that is more nuanced and involves negotiating indiscriminate memories, personal deficiencies, uncontrolled trauma, being unmoved by trauma, or remaining in the stigmatised difference.

One way out of this particular 'credibility conundrum' could be that proposed by Woodiwiss (2014). She suggests there is a need to separate innocence from credibility so that all experiences of sexual violence are recognised regardless of the individual's conformity to sexual innocence. She also suggests the need to separate wrongfulness from harm so that sexual violence is accepted as condemnable irrespective of the

DOI: 10.1057/9781137461728.0004

presentation of distress. However, with women's accounts in mind, it is imperative that credibility itself is troubled, as part of the categorising process to 'rape victim' identification. Otherwise the symbolic violence encountered when called into this subjectivity cannot be averted. Sexual violence is perceived as inevitably and visibly traumatic requiring specialist support, but the majority of women who have experienced sexual violence tell no one (Women's Resource Centre 2008). Maybe in not telling, or avoiding defining their experiences as sexual violence, women are creating an opportunity to circumvent credibility assessment and rejecting the inevitable destruction to identity that acceptance of trauma necessitates.

DOI: 10.1057/9781137461728.0004

4
Responsibility

Abstract: *Chapter 4 examines the cultural presumption that blames women for sexual violence. Originally, feminism attempted to absolve women of their responsibility but denounced their agency. Women's accounts of 'complicity', mothers' denial, and female perpetration necessitate a more robust engagement with female sexual agency particularly. Kelly's theorisation of relative powerlessness (1997a) offers an alternative that does not trivialise, sensationalise, or excuse female-perpetrated abuse, but situates female agency within differential power relations. However, women's accounts spotlight the role of others and the usually invisible perpetrator, so this theory is extended to recognise the responsibility of wider society in the reiteration of sexual violence.*

Healicon, Alison. *The Politics of Sexual Violence: Rape, Identity and Feminism.* Basingstoke: Palgrave Macmillan, 2015. DOI: 10.1057/9781137461728.0005.

DOI: 10.1057/9781137461728.0005

Three people were involved because, like, you know, I was basically (raped) in a park with this guy and these two other men, that I thought were basically gonna help me, came (over and watched) and even though they didn't do anything... I've felt a lot more you know, bitterness and anger and resentment towards them than I did towards the person, the other person who was there (and who raped me).

In a way I can possibly, possibly think perhaps even if it was rape, perhaps, there can have been some blurring of the lines, some misunderstanding on his part... but I know that that wasn't there for them (who watched)... I feel that if it had just been this one person... my recovery would have been a lot better (but) because there were two other people there (watching), and also that thinking that they were going to help, and just getting... the worst rejection, you know that has affected my whole view of the world.

(Ruby)

Sexual violence involves not only the perpetrator and the 'victim' but exists in a social context with multiple sites of relative responsibility. Women who have experienced sexual violence assume responsibility because they have assessed themselves defective or complicit and there are no culturally viable alternatives. Yet these intimate acts of power and control occur, and are made meaningful, in gendered interrelationships which ultimately and inevitably blame or vilify women. Meanwhile the perpetrator remains elusive and peripheral and the role of others in sexual violence is obfuscated. Nonetheless, others are involved in incidences of sexual violence both actively and explicitly through participation, observation, and trivialisation but also implicitly through denial, avoidance, ignorance, and indifference. The explicit and implicit involvement of others compounds experiences of sexual violence and further complicates the emotional and physical impact of abuse, but this involvement of others is in practice overlooked and under-theorised. Sexual violence as a social issue is neglected at the expense of scrutinising the actions and character of the 'victim'. As such, responsibility and the ensuing blame are readily attached to the woman.

Women who have experienced sexual violence feel complicit in their abuse and blame themselves. Therefore, it is necessary to consider

DOI: 10.1057/9781137461728.0005

responsibility more broadly as it is produced in the intra-actions of bodies, social spaces, structures, and language. That is, in order to refigure a just way of articulating and understanding her feelings of complicity that does not produce her as victim or villain, the role and participation of others within the social and cultural context has to be examined. Consideration of responsibility as a collective and gendered dynamic, rather than personal duty, might facilitate an understanding of abuse which enables women to make sense of their involvement devoid of blame and without relinquishing agency. It may also bring to the fore the role of the perpetrator-and-others.

This chapter considers issues of responsibility by firstly exploring implications of certain feminist theory that attempts to absolve women of blame and shame but which requires positioning women as passive victims both of specific incidents of violence and of generalised gendered social roles. Secondly, the cultural vilification of female-perpetrated sexual abuse is considered here as this debate demonstrates the consequences and dangers inherent in gendered assumptions and roles that rely on a lack of female (sexual) agency and which ultimately operate to reinforce and reproduce victim/woman blaming, further obscuring responsibility in sexual violence. Thirdly, sexual violence as collective social responsibility, indicated above in the explicit conjunction of 'perpetrator-and-others', is considered as it is articulated in accounts from women interviewed in this study, thus emphasising the need to incorporate the implicit and explicit role of others.

Feminism and responsibility

Feminism has theorised male violence against women in conjunction with grass roots feminist activism that located this abuse of male power in a social and political context and provided practical opportunities for escape and transformation. The theories of two main protagonists, Brownmiller (1975) and MacKinnon (1989; 1995), are considered here as they typically and specifically consider rape within the context of the oppression of women and gendered power relations that had immediate implications for praxis and whose legacy continues. Both theorists provided an alternative to victim blaming mythology in their assertion that male oppression, encompassed in cultural and social structures, causes sexual violence. However, it is argued here that their underlying

DOI: 10.1057/9781137461728.0005

assumption positions women as passive and biologically subordinate, and as such their theories are unable to grapple with the intricacies of sexual violence including the role of others. Women accept responsibility and blame because they sought out, talked, or joked with the perpetrator, complied to avert violence or death, and attempted strategies to temper an escalating situation. Sexual violence involves others as observers, planners, facilitators, or blamers. In their denial of female agency, and ignorance of the involvement of others, complex issues of responsibility are insufficiently articulated.

In *Against Our Will* Brownmiller (1975) proposed a political theory of stranger rape to counter persistent myths that assumed rape was motivated by a dangerous and rapacious female sexuality, which transfixed men, unable to stop their natural desire, once initiated. Advocating parity before the law with other incidents of physical violence, Brownmiller severed rape as violence from sex, promoting the significance of rape as physical assault rather than a sexual encounter. Arguing that rape was violence and not sex rendered irrelevant the sexuality of the individual woman and female sexuality more generally. As such she exposed the brutality of rape that had been concealed behind this assumption of 'just bad sex' and a female sexuality that required guarding against and for which women were responsible. Moreover, Brownmiller situated rape within a system of oppression, where power is universally located within the male class. This political belief is encapsulated in Brownmiller's (1975: 15) eponymous phrase: rape is 'nothing more or less than a conscious process of intimidation in which all men keep all women in a state of fear'. In practice situating rape as violence by the male class meant that self-blame could be alleviated. For women who felt they had put themselves in a dangerous position, or who wondered why they had been targeted particularly, this theorisation provided a counterargument that claimed it was not the woman's fault as responsibility for rape lay with men. Rape happened not because of who they were as individuals but was a fate that women as a class could experience and as such were effected by collectively.

Brownmiller divorced sex from violence in order to promote rape as a serious and brutal crime. But for MacKinnon (1995: 29) sex is central to our understanding of rape, suggesting that:

> so long as we say these things are abuses of violence, not sex, we fail to criticise what has been made of sex, what has been done to us *through* sex, because we leave the link between rape and intercourse, sexual harassment and sex roles, pornography and eroticism, right where it is.

DOI: 10.1057/9781137461728.0005

To suggest that rape is not about sex is for MacKinnon a disavowal of the fundamental way in which society is constructed unequally according to sexual differences. Whilst Brownmiller proposed a dualism of gendered classes, MacKinnon employed Rich's (1980) concept of compulsory heterosexuality as the organising system of contemporary society through which gender inequality is maintained. Compulsory heterosexuality, as it is forced upon us, is defined primarily as a dynamic of masculine sexual domination and feminine sexual passivity and submission. Rape is not simply about lack of consent as within heterosexual sex a certain amount of force is considered normal and abuse is an inevitable expression of the male sex drive. Rather, MacKinnon (1989: 172) suggests that 'if sexuality is central to women's definition and forced sex is central to sexuality, rape is indigenous, not exceptional, to women's social condition'. In compulsory heterosexuality female sexuality is defined in relation to the power of masculine domination and is inevitably passive. Thus, heterosex is impossible to resist and contrary to women's interest and rape is an inevitable expression of heterosex, legitimated in culture and social institutions that deny the existence of an alternative and active female sexuality. Such a theory justified feminist campaigns that challenged institutional, cultural, and political assumptions and practices and rendered impossible women's responsibility for rape.

Situating sexual violence within wider political injustices is important theoretically and practically, in highlighting the social significance of rape and sexual abuse and in the alleviation of blame and shame for individual women. In this feminism, it is impossible for women to be responsible for sexual violence as it is an inevitable consequence of the social and structural reproduction of oppression. Unfortunately, whilst responsibility is located with men as a class, in these theorisations, women are automatically denied agency, merely victims of gendered and oppressive circumstance. Moreover, responsibility and blame are located elsewhere precisely because women are denied an active sexuality, and this has serious repercussions for women who question their involvement in their own abuse. If women are denied sexual agency to remove blame, certain experiences of sexual violence are silenced. Amy describes clearly the need to be able to make sense of her participation in the abuse she experienced as a child:

> because I liked the feeling I got from what he was doing, using his hand basically and I got a nice feeling... so I actually encouraged it by putting his hand there and stuff. So that's where the guilt creeps in because I feel like

DOI: 10.1057/9781137461728.0005

I'm a dirty sort of tart or slag. And no matter how much counselling I get I can't shake that feeling because I encouraged it. Although people tell me it wasn't me, I'd been groomed .... He was buying me, sort of thing and I know that but it was normal to me and ... I still can't get past that guilt.

Amy suggests there is a need to name and debate the sex of abuse neither by prioritising violence (Brownmiller 1975) nor in response to an aggressive male sexuality (MacKinnon 1989). She also notes that in practice recovery involves acceptance of an inevitable victimisation in order to relinquish responsibility and grasp a modicum of credibility. Any participation by the girl/woman is interpreted as a consequence of her powerlessness not only in that situation of abuse but because she is female and/or young. Brison (2002: 93) argues that 'sex' of sexual violence matters because 'it is violence committed (typically) on the basis of sex (or because of the sex of the victim)'. Also men who rape describe it as sexually motivated, a means to sexual access that would otherwise be denied to them (Scully and Morolla 1995). Therefore, Amy is suggesting that an articulation of sex within rape and abuse is much more than being a casualty of a sexually dominant and powerful class or one that requires relinquishing agency to a(n older) predatory male. Amy is concerned to understand her own sexual agency in order to make sense of responsibility, and the theories from Brownmiller and MacKinnon which rely on a passive and victimised female sexuality are insufficient for such analysis. Rejecting sex for violence prevents dialogue necessary to appreciate situations where women feel sexually complicit and responsible, which is further compounded in rhetoric that female sexuality is defined only in response to male sexual aggression. The 'sex' of sexual violence is central but not only because it is a cultural expression of gendered stratification. Sexual violence involves socially designated sexual body parts and such violation is intimately and shamefully experienced. It is both sexualised and violence. Therefore, to understand the intricacies and impact of sexual violence in practice necessitates analysis which engages with an active female sexuality whilst questioning the inevitability of victim blaming and includes acknowledgement of the role of others.

Theorising female perpetrators

Victim blaming rape mythology links automatically an, albeit distorted, active female sexuality with fault and responsibility. To counter this,

DOI: 10.1057/9781137461728.0005

some feminist theorisation would rather assert the powerlessness of girls and women and ignore the involvement of others in situations of abuse to absolve women of responsibility. Women who may feel complicit in their own experiences of abuse are unable to articulate this because there is no space in which to engage with such 'participation' as women are either without sexuality or blamed for their sexuality. Certain experiences of abuse therefore cannot be thoroughly known and are accounted for instead through gendered assumptions, which in practice render support services inaccessible. Nowhere is this more demonstrable than the theorisation of the role of female perpetrators in sexual violence who are signified differently from other women and demonised in comparison with male perpetrators, leaving women abused by women with little critical understanding or societal support. Whether women sexually abuse or facilitate abuse, they attract societal vitriol. But neither rape mythology that blames female sexuality nor the powerless victim of feminism is helpful to women trying to make sense of their responsibility in experiences of sexual violence involving women and especially mothers.

Whilst there has been a burgeoning interest in violent women, including those who abuse men and children, there is negligible feminist theorisation, an unfortunate gap given the need to make sense of female-perpetrated abuse and responsibility. In the interviews conducted for this study three women noted particularly various forms of abuse by their mothers. This section focuses on these particular experiences in order to trouble the duality of the evil and sexually aberrant or sexless and nurturing mother to articulate a more nuanced consideration of sexual violence. The following accounts are rich and reveal the intricacies of lives that are well in excess of the essence encapsulated in the following argument.

> It was the women in the family that were the perpetrators, the ring leaders, and that going off with the men to be raped was preferable to being left with the women. (Caitlin)

> You get abused on a night and nobody sits having breakfast the next morning acknowledging what happened and so you grow up with a sense that that didn't happen, it reinforces the dissociation. And the mother that was either complicit in the abuse or directly involved in the abuse the night before is then giving you your packed lunch for school and taking care of you and making sure that you're dressed properly and you're warm enough for school. So there's a tenderness and care, 'make sure you've got your gloves',

DOI: 10.1057/9781137461728.0005

whilst a few hours previously there's extreme stuff going on, you're being tortured by her…. It's this mind control aspect of mothering that … is one of the most pervasive, damaging effects of it all, isn't it? Not so much the rape but how you've been made to believe that that didn't happen. (Caitlin)

I strongly suspect my mother was DID (Dissociative Identity Disorder) as well, because she just seemed so many different people and so I think I am more messed up by the fact that sometimes she was nice than that most of the time she was nasty. Just get on and be horrible the whole time cos then I know who you are. (Caitlin)

I think (my mum did know about the abuse) but I don't think she cared. I'm not being funny but there was somebody came into our house…. This bloke was sent up to sleep in me sister's bedroom and he raped her…. And when she told mum next morning, cos she was stuck, his arms were around her and she couldn't move, she was awake all night. And when she told me mum. 'So it takes two to tango', me mother told her. But I think he paid me mum. To have some money, cos she was desperate for money. (Amy)

And (my mother) was naked and we were in bed together and she told me also to undress fully and I was like a zombie, I did that and she hugged me and I had nightmares about how she is doing something sexually to me and in the middle of the night I couldn't sleep and I left…. But then after this it makes me laugh, but on the other side I think it has to be painful, but I don't feel this pain I just think they were crazy and I didn't have enough experience, but if you think properly, it is some kind of abuse. She didn't have to put me naked in her bed and hug me. It's crazy, you know. (Victoria)

In an email after this interview Victoria suggests that:

This is the hardest for me – my mother could shout at me for no reason for hours, swear at me, say such humiliating words which do not exist in English … she could threaten to kill me, hit my head with the fists and order me to stop crying otherwise she'd kill me or it would kill her and I'd be guilty in her death … but other moments she could be very warm, not even to notice the things I did not do – like washing dishes, etc., she could be very caring, loving … even incisive about what I need, she could make me happy, but then again … the hell came back and she became a beast … dragging me by hair through the long corridor of our flat….

It is clear from the pain expressed in these excerpts that it is more difficult to make sense of abuse when mothers are involved. Although victimisation by some of the men in their lives was necessarily distressing, their mother's complicity meant they were confronted with experiences of abuse that challenge the social certainty that women are naturally

DOI: 10.1057/9781137461728.0005

and essentially reliable and nurturing. It is presumed that mothers will believe, protect, and prevent such occurrences. That men perpetrate sexual violence is considered normal or inevitable almost and constitutive of behaviour within boundaries that signify masculinity. Yet, abusive women defy not only biological definition but also societal assumptions of woman/motherhood. Amy's mother was physically violent towards her, gave her up to local authority care, and set up the situation in which her sister was raped and Amy yearned for 'real parents' to love and care for her. For Caitlin and Victoria the barrier to making sense of their experiences was the inconsistency of the care from mothers who both attended to their needs as children and abused them. These mothers did not provide the unselfish and permanent nurturing that biology and society assume. They were also involved in their daughter's sexual abuse, causing significant distress and confusion. The predominant circulating sexual violence narrative of predatory male and vulnerable female victim cannot be relied upon to explain such abuse, and so women abused by women flounder, unable to comprehend their experiences. Instead, negotiating and engaging with the contemporary cultural imagination which sensationalises and categorises women who abuse as deviant, social pariahs existing outside of acceptable feminine boundaries and far worse than their male counterpart.

There is little theorisation to challenge this cultural vilification of women who abuse as research tends to focus on the identification of individual personality deficiencies and psychological typologies (Matthews et al. 1989; Grayston and DeLuca 1999; Vandiver and Kercher 2004), rather than locate such abuse in social situations of inequality. In studies that do notionally acknowledge the significance of gender, women are constructed as mentally ill, poorly socialised, subject to domestic pressures, with a high level of physical, emotional, and sexual abuse in their past histories. It is also suggested that women victimise children in conjunction with a (usually) male accomplice, or are so poor they sell their children for sex (Kaufman et al. 1995: Grattagliano et al. 2012). Just as Peter (2006, 2008) found in her research of mother-daughter sexual abuse, there is evidence here of the application of such theories. Caitlin and Amy thought their mothers were victims of their previous experiences of abuse, had mental ill health, and colluded because they were controlled by male perpetrators. Amy's mother was financially destitute. As well as ascribing 'mad' or 'victim' to their mothers, Peter (2006) suggests daughters also saw their mothers as 'bad', again evidenced here. As

DOI: 10.1057/9781137461728.0005

Victoria says: 'I could not see her as an insane person 'cause she was functioning very successfully and she was a famous (artist) ... acknowledged by authoritative people.' Amy asks: 'What had I ever done to her? I know she suffered abuse 'cause somebody told me years later, but why did it make her want to take it out on me?' In attempts to understand mother-perpetrated abuse each woman draws on cultural tropes that suggest such mothers are either mad or victims of circumstance and occasionally bad. As they grapple with their mothers as abhorrent sexual predators or powerless victims, the daughters' confusion demonstrates that these categorisations are insufficient and engaged with problematically.

At the heart of the insufficiency in these rationalisations of female-perpetrated abuse is the readiness to attribute responsibility to the 'evil' mother without critique of the depth of gendered assumptions. Whilst male perpetrators are not generally held responsible, women who abuse are disproportionately vilified and demonised because their psychology is so divergent from what is considered appropriately female. Yet at the same time because abuse by women is culturally alien and too terrible, it is rather trivialised or misconstrued and consequently goes unrecognised or unnamed. So, women who are 'mad' or 'bad' are considered responsible as they are evidencing a socially unacceptable and active sexuality. Whilst explanations which suggest women are 'mad' or 'victims' frustrate analysis by writing off the significance of such abuse by mothers. Neither position, located in gendered assumptions, is useful for understanding responsibility in sexual violence. Moreover, such theorisation condensed around the duality of the abhorrent or victim mother underestimates the complexity of mother-perpetrated abuse, not only for daughters making sense of their experiences, but also for practitioners who, due to the lack of alternative theorisation, respond with judgement and disbelief.

Just as Caitlin, Victoria, and Amy articulate, women who have experienced abuse by their mothers engage with and negotiate popular cultural conceptions of motherhood to understand the complexity of their experience. Denov (2004) suggests that in order to ease the conflict and discomfort that perceiving their mothers as evil would prompt, women attempt to understand abuse within the usual ideation of motherhood to redefine abuse as an (albeit adverse) extension of mothering. Thus, socially abhorrent and frightening realities are transformed into more harmless, but psychologically containable, experiences. However, Denov also suggests that this societal perception of the nurturing asexual mother leads to reluctance among professionals to accept abuse involving female

DOI: 10.1057/9781137461728.0005

perpetrators. Just as individuals negotiate the predominant theoretical construction which 'excuses' abusive mothers' behaviour, workers in the field continue to use existing and accepted frameworks which rely on stereotypes of female sexual passivity even when critical of them (Fitzroy 2001), resulting in disbelief, trivialisation, and judgement. The perceived threat abusive mothers pose to society silences women abused by women, forecloses opportunities to consider more critically the situation in which mothers abuse, and effectively excludes women from support.

If abuse by mothers is so vilified, because female sexual agency is culturally and theoretically denied, silencing the articulation and recognition of certain experiences, responsibility in abuse is further obfuscated and inevitably gendered. In recovery, women who feel complicit accept their powerlessness and lack of sexual agency in order to be freed from responsibility, whilst women who abuse are in excess of a dangerous and evil sexuality. Either way, women abused by women, or who feel 'complicit', are alienated from meaningful comprehension of their experiences, and responsibility remains uncritically attached to the 'victim' noted above by Amy. For Victoria, the difficulty in making sense of abuse by her mother was compounded when she sought support from disbelieving agencies, resulting in confusion and self-blame. In her own mind Victoria felt she had misconstrued the situation with her mother because there are few and only restrictive cultural tropes with which to articulate abuse by mothers, and this was confirmed in agency disbelief and denial of support. This insufficiency in analysis suggests the need for theorisation of female sexual agency that tempers the vilification of mothers and women who abuse and facilitates the articulation of abuse by women and of 'complicity' in a way that negates gendered assumptions so that issues of responsibility are adequately considered. Such analysis also necessitates theorisation of the role of others, including organisational response, as allocation of responsibility is not only personally negotiated but is externally reinforced in various ways.

Others' responsibility

Female-perpetrated violence opens up discussion to include analysis of the role of women in abuse and highlights gendered explanations which confuse issues of responsibility and inculcate self-blame. Furthermore, accounts from women suggest there are multiple sites of responsibility

DOI: 10.1057/9781137461728.0005

necessitating a reconsideration that incorporates recognition of the role of others, including the perpetrator, as well as social and collective responsibility. It is in relations with others, which Butler (2004: 21) refers to as 'the crucible of social life', that self-blame is either reinforced or averted and responsibility assigned. This section attempts such a reconsideration of responsibility by concentrating on themes that arose in specific accounts from women interviewed.

The previous chapter evidenced the difficulties in disclosing abuse as it involves negotiating victimhood and credibility. This section firstly considers disclosing abuse particularly to non-abusive mothers to demonstrate that even when women are not involved in abuse they are systematically blamed and held responsible. But in these accounts also significant is the need to be believed, especially by mothers, thus introducing the idea that we are all implicitly involved in sexual violence if we respond with disbelief and perpetuate rape mythology. Secondly, Kelly's theory of sexual violence (1997a, 1997b; Kelly and Radford 1997) is considered. Unlike Brownmiller (1975) and MacKinnon (1989, 1995), Kelly provides a framework of relative powerlessness in which female-perpetrated abuse and gendered assumptions are acknowledged and through which the complexity of, and responsibility within, sexual violence can be articulated. However, this theory, located in a context hostile to feminism and feminist praxis, continues to preserve the powerlessness of women. So finally drawing on interview excerpts, an extension to this framework is proposed to include more specifically the role of others in the perpetuation of sexual violence and social responsibility in order to remove responsibility from the individual without the inevitable acceptance of victimisation.

It has already been suggested in the previous chapter that disclosure involves acceptance of the role of 'victim' and invites assessment of the individual's credibility. However, the following excerpts demonstrate that revealing abuse to their mothers was experienced by the women in this study as particularly complicated and more risky than disclosing to friends or even agencies. When Victoria disclosed to her mother the sexual abuse by her father, she recalls,

> the first three days (my mother) believed and then she denied it. 'He died, it can't be like this, he can't protect himself, he can't justify himself, he's dead in heaven, how can you blame such a person, it could be cruel. This psychotherapist put this wrong idea (into your head) because they want to use you for money.'

Dawn and Maya describe their concerns about disclosure to their mothers:

> In a way I don't want her to be worried by what's going on, but more than that I don't want to say anything to her, cos I don't want the same reaction again. It took an awful long time for me to say yes there is a problem, yes I need help. It sounds really arrogant but I've always been the one people turn to for help but that's the way it's been and for me to say help, takes one heck of a lot of doing. And for somebody then to say you shouldn't need that help is... can't deal with that especially not when it comes from my mum. So I'm just not going to put myself in that position. (Dawn)

> I cannot be sure my mother knew at the time. Though she must have. Everyone else realised. And she was around me a lot more than them too. She certainly did nothing when I spoke up in 'family therapy' as a teenager. She kept her mouth shut. And she stopped attending and went into hospital as her diabetes suddenly 'went' out of control. I think she needed to have a distraction as she couldn't stand up to any of these truths and wanted everything to go away. It was a given in my family that if you stand up to my father with truths, you are going to be totally rejected, humiliated, ridiculed, ousted, dumped, dropped.... Speaking out as a child left me desperate. I know now how my mother loved me, but she just couldn't stick her neck out over this. (Maya)

> I did try to tell my mum which was quite a big thing, my counsellor said try to tell her and she didn't react very well and that she tried to deny what I was telling her, she just didn't, brushed, glazed over it and pretended that I wasn't trying to tell her something important. I'm not angry towards her. To be honest it was a massive weight off my shoulders because well I've totally done my responsibility, I've tried to tell you, I don't feel guilty anymore, but at the same time, you know I do feel that she let me down, because I didn't tell her properly or coherently, I was sort of trying to tell her, but I know if I had a daughter I would be making her tell me. *(Alison: yes you'd know there was something enough to ask a bit.)* Well she did ask me some things like 'did you call the police' and stuff like that but she just couldn't handle it. (Ruby)

The mother-daughter interaction is crucial in determining self-blame and responsibility. To have sexual violence recognised in all its severity by her mother is both expected and yet not assumed. As such, motherly acceptance can relieve individuals of responsibility, making this particular moment of disclosure fearfully anticipated and particularly risky. Indeed, in most of the accounts here this fear was justified as mothers' responses left women feeling astonished, disappointed, blamed, and ultimately rejected. As noted in these excerpts, the fear of not being believed,

DOI: 10.1057/9781137461728.0005

of having their experiences trivialised or written off, and of questioning their need for support, could prevent women from disclosing to their mothers, foreclosing opportunities to disclose to others. After all, if your mother doesn't believe you, then who else will? Other concerns include protecting their mothers from the disgust and pain that rape elicits, or questioning their mother's allegiance especially when the perpetrator is another family member. These disclosures reveal the underlying assumption that because of their gender and role, women and mothers, particularly, are supposed to have an inherent connection to their daughters and an understanding of what it feels like to be a victim of gendered inequality. As such, it is necessarily assumed that women, particularly mothers, are supportive. The cultural ideation of the nurturing mother conceals the appropriation of rape myth acceptance and when confronted with the converse situation, women feel blamed, responsible, and without adequate explanation with which to make sense of their experiences and their mother's rejection.

Many women decide not to disclose sexual violence to their mothers to protect them from what they feel to be the repellent truth, and because they fear their mother's rejection, thus avoiding jeopardising the cultural assumption of the nurturing mother and a confrontation with their mother's active reproduction of rape mythology. Maya's comments are useful here as they illustrate clearly the process of making sense of abuse and her mother's responses to it. As noted in her comments above, Maya was rejected by her mother in her lack of acknowledgement of the abuse Maya experienced as a child in the home. Rather than being forthrightly critical of her mother, though, Maya attempted to understand the context in which this abuse and the subsequent disclosure took place. Just as Denov (2004) suggested earlier, abuse by mothers is often redefined in order to preserve traditional gender stereotypes of the idealised mother so as to reduce the emotional impact that such abuse can cause. Similarly, Maya has to consider her mother's response in terms of her powerlessness within the family in order to manage the distress that her rejection on disclosure invokes. However, in her comments, Maya pinpoints exactly the need for adequate theorisation of the role of mothers and others and their responses, which situates rape myth acceptance in a gendered cultural context in order to then facilitate understanding of the impact such responses cause and to negate blame and responsibility.

The effects of mothers' responses to disclosures of child sexual abuse particularly have been considered in feminist texts in order to challenge

DOI: 10.1057/9781137461728.0005

mother-blaming assumptions and to introduce some theorisation of the impact of sexual violence on the mother-daughter dynamic. Rather than assume mother's collusion in abuse, or attribute blame to her deficiencies as a wife, the damage to mother-daughter relationships is situated within patriarchy and powerlessness to identify a complex range of responses and barriers confronting mothers of daughters abused in the family. Behind some of these unhelpful and harmful responses, cited by the women interviewed here, Taylor-Johnson (1992) found that mothers were often overwhelmed with the contradictory demands made of them subsequent to disclosure and feelings of having let their daughter down whilst professionals apportioned them with blame. Bolen (2003) argues that historically mother-blaming has become so established within social services that non abusive mothers continue to be actively constructed as participating in the abuse and for Plummer and Eastin (2007) are perceived as blameworthy for not keeping their daughter safe or for choosing an incestuous partner. Thus, mothers were not only blamed but also blamed themselves, even though they did not participate in the actual abuse.

Croghan and Miell (1995) meanwhile considered explanations from daughters who blamed their non-abusive mothers for not protecting them from their abuser. They proffer a framework of meaning based on the idealised social construction and appropriation of the 'normal family', through which daughters interpreted their experiences of abuse. Non-abusing mothers were therefore blamed for their inadequacies because they failed to match up to behaviour other daughters could expect from their 'real' but ideal mothers, who would protect at all costs. Revealed are very different expectations applied to the male perpetrator and non-abusive mothers. Whilst male abusers were excused on the basis of their adverse early experiences or existing stress, adult daughters abused in childhood expected more from their relationships with their mothers and were more censorious of their mother's behaviour. In practice these feminist texts which focused on the mother-daughter dynamic highlighted embedded gendered attitudes to challenge women-blaming practices within support organisations. They also provided an alternative perspective to enable both mothers and daughters to understand how they were caught up in a situation not of their own making. However, in order to challenge gendered assumptions that situate responsibility for abuse with daughters and mothers, these writers ultimately deny complexity because they position women as unfortunate and powerless victims of a system that privileges male power.

DOI: 10.1057/9781137461728.0005

Kelly, a leading feminist writer and activist in the field of sexual violence in the UK, has developed a theory that facilitates the articulation of complex experiences, thereby challenging gendered assumptions that situate responsibility for sexual violence with women and girls. Instead of locating responsibility for sexual violence either within the psychology of the individual (woman) or within a system of male privilege that victimises an already submissive class of women, Kelly's theory of relative powerlessness acknowledges a more complicated power dynamic. Based on the work of black feminists especially, who advocated scepticism of patriarchy as the sole oppressor of women, Kelly suggests that sexual violence is experienced at the intersection of gender, race, sexuality, disability, and class. Whilst such institutional oppression exerts considerable influence, it is in the milieu of competing and conflicting oppression that individual agency emerges. For Kelly (1997a: 37) 'gender [is] a social construct which recognises the variability with which gendered selves and individual biography combine' without reducing all forms of 'power plays' to institutionalised structures of power. Rather than suggest all women are victimised similarly, this theorisation enables consideration of differing experiences situated in varying power relations. In this theorisation, agentic individuals purposively exercise power, albeit necessarily gendered and constrained within complex intersections of oppression.

This more nuanced conceptualisation of sexual violence as operating within complex interrelations of power allows for a consideration of the severity of female-perpetrated violence and 'complicity', whether that involves women in abuse, negative responses to disclosure, or as it is articulated by women who have experienced sexual violence. Implicit to this framework is an understanding that responsibility for sexual violence is ultimately explained within gendered social relations, the purpose of which for Kelly (1997a: 348) is social control. As such, although both men and women abuse, there are considerable differences in terms of scale, cause, impact, and attitudes because of the ontological experience of oppression and epistemologically in the cultural production of knowledge about sexual violence. Female-perpetrated abuse then is situated within the context of gendered social relations and other forms of oppression, and although distressing, the moments which women have 'power over' are connected to, and can be explained in, their powerlessness generally as women in society and within the specifics of their family relations and personal histories. This is not to excuse

DOI: 10.1057/9781137461728.0005

female-perpetrated abuse as a consequence of powerlessness, nor does it absolve female perpetrators of responsibility as victims of oppression. Rather, Kelly suggests (1997a: 40), 'being victimised does not remove all responsibility, but it places actions and choices in a particular, constrained context'. Thus female-perpetrated violence is experientially different because it operates within different power relations than male-perpetrated violence and is perceived differently as evidenced within rape mythology and social attitudes to sexual violence. Unlike other theories that rendered women victims of circumstance, female-perpetrated abuse and complicity are understood as the enactment of agency within situations of relative powerlessness.

Kelly's work is particularly significant as she recognised at an early stage the impact of neglecting both theoretically and practically female-perpetrated violence. Kelly (1997a: 35) argued that 'if we fail to develop a feminist analysis of abuse by women we are handing over the issue to the professionals and the media. Silence also means that we will continue to fail women and children who have suffered at the hands of women.' Such warnings recognised that women's use of violence was perceived as a direct challenge to traditional feminist analyses and practice strategies. In voicing the issue, Kelly exposed some reluctance within feminism to consider female-perpetrated violence because it supposed a rewriting of theory, especially political, in light of contemporary hostility towards feminism. Whilst popular feminist backlash questioned the scale of violence against women, feminist organisations were seen as politically motivated, and gender neutral-policy demanded the inclusion of men in women-only services. The fear, therefore, that the issue of female violence would be used to undermine the 'grudging acceptance' (Kelly 1997a: 35) of the scale of male violence was (and remains) considerable. However, it was precisely because of these challenges that feminism had to confront the issue of female violence, but it did so by adapting rather than radicalising established analyses.

Kelly's theorisation that recognised the impact of compounding oppression and gendered relations is significant in understanding abuse perpetrated by women, rejection by mothers on disclosure of abuse, and issues of complicity, but there remains a tendency to reduce women to powerless victims even though there is an acknowledgement of relativity within the constraints of multiple oppressions. As such the notion of a restricted agency only notionally engages with the complexity of social responsibility including the role of others in sexual violence. The

DOI: 10.1057/9781137461728.0005

following extracts evocatively articulate multiple sites of responsibility to suggest that responsibility is not simply a matter of assessing a definitive truth about who is blameworthy or blameless. *Rather, each elucidates the need for detailed analysis of the incident moment by moment to acknowledge a diversity of points at which power was contested.* Rape mythology has been and continues to be challenged in feminism, but clearly noted in accounts from women is the need to analyse more thoroughly the role of others and collective responsibility. Firstly, Donna describes here a situation some years ago when she decided to report her experiences of rape to the police in Europe where it occurred:

> So I felt quite within my rights to go to the police and report this incident and they did the worst thing possible which was they got him in and they sat us both in the same room, while I told my story and they looked at him and they were all sniggering. And they sent me for a medical and because there was no bruising it was thrown away 'you're just full of crap' basically and I felt doubly violated with that I really did and I felt like nobody's going to listen to this, nobody is going to take me (seriously), see my side…. And I don't think it was the first time he'd done that and probably not the last. And it wouldn't surprise me if the police were involved as well, really because they knew him. They knew exactly who he was and they had to get him in and they were chatting like old friends. It sickens me. (Donna)

> Within a ritual abuse setting, you've got a whole circle of people watching and not doing anything about it and I think there is something particularly horrific about that because you've got the aggressor and you put aside why they are doing what they are doing, but then you've got people who aren't acting out some violence they're just watching and I think that then brings it into 'will anybody help if I go for help or will they standby as well?' Something incredibly dehumanising about somebody watching you be raped, that all the things that we expect to kick in, you know compassion and empathy and intervention, don't and that I think really destroys your faith in then any services helping. (Caitlin)

> (after being raped at 15 at a party by her boyfriend) I remember someone taking me home, I think it was someone's parents and I was made to feel I was in the wrong because I was drunk. Nobody mentioned anything about what happened in the bedroom and so neither did I. I was too embarrassed. (Donna)

> I did tell J, my school friend when I was about 12. I went to hospital at 14 and then again at 15 (with anorexia). The second time J's mother rang the hospital and informed them of what I had told J a few years previously because they thought I might well die and that the knowledge of abuse might be a

DOI: 10.1057/9781137461728.0005

key for me to get well. There is a tiny reference scribble in the nurse's day notes. But that's all. I had the same shrink as before and no-one took any notice of J's mum's call. (Maya)

The shrink(s) believed my father's cover-up lies, which was devastating for me. My shrink was a woman and she couldn't hear that I was abused. (Nor could any of the others either though. Or the social worker.) Having people who were meant to rescue me believe my father was very damaging for me. My shrink dismissed me in my sessions from 14–16 years. She believed my father's cover up when he said the incest was 'games'... I then spent the rest of those years practically silent. I did make one more effort to be heard. I wrote the shrink a letter. By that time I was taking responsibility for the abuse in the letter, because aren't games a 50-50 shared thing? Like tennis or chess. And I like games so I must have been a bad girl. (Maya)

J (her mother) knocked Amy black and blue, that's all that was in me file, the bit that I got to see. So why didn't they take me off her? (Amy)

In these extracts, the process to responsibility is exposed as more complex than suggested in reductionist theories which absolve female blame by presupposing the guilt of all men or in terms of relative powerlessness. Alongside self-blame, other sites of responsibility are apparent – rapists, observers, listeners, and professionals whose actions together sanction abuse and consequently silence and blame sexually violated women. There are two levels of complicity here which highlight responsibility as collective and socially produced. Firstly, there is the passive but nevertheless collusive involvement of others evidenced in the form of observation, inaction, disbelief, and ignorance. Observers in ritual abuse, or bystanders in the park, or friends and practitioners who choose not to mention what they heard, or hear what is said, ignore the realities of sexual violence for the individual woman. In so doing they send an unambiguous message that no help is available. Such inaction suggests that no one is prepared to step in to confront sexual violence because it is legitimate and the 'victim' does not matter. It is almost as if in their passive acceptance of rape, their responsibility and participation does not register as it is assumed that blame inevitably lies with the woman. Ruby, quoted at the beginning of this chapter, and Caitlin acknowledge completely the helplessness of their situation and therefore readily blame, and feel more aggrieved by, the inaction of observers. The behaviour of the rapist could be explained with albeit inadequate theories about misreading signals, but collective responsibility, standing back and allowing it to happen, is much harder to explain away.

DOI: 10.1057/9781137461728.0005

The second level of complicity involves a more proactive participant, whose actions deliberately contribute to the sexual violence situation itself or to the dehumanising disregard of the woman in her disclosure. Such complicity is evidenced in the time, effort, and thought on the part of many people in the planning and execution of sexual violence as in Caitlin's experiences of ritual abuse. It is also evidenced within the institutional embodiment of rape mythology where agencies actively condone sexual violence, described by Donna. Participants including organisers, perpetrators, and collusive practitioners are supported in their actions within institutions and agencies whose ethos accepts rape as the responsibility of the woman/'victim'. Situations are contrived to facilitate sexual violence and in conjunction with agencies that operate to actively undermine women's right to be heard. Together these elements of complicity render unaccountable those responsible because they work to silence women who have nowhere to go. This contrivance of situations which functions to deflect responsibility away from these proactive participants is also clearly evident in the actions of the rapists themselves.

The proactive behaviour of the perpetrator ought to be identifiable as evidence of clear responsibility. Yet for women making sense of responsibility, the role of the perpetrator is problematic. In a study which considered the location of blame in abuse, Reavey and Gough (2000) found that women were not only more likely to blame themselves, but scant reference was made to the perpetrator at all in discussion about responsibility. In the above excerpts it is apparent that women were more ready to question the roles of observers and practitioners than the abusers, suggesting there is some difficulty in determining the perpetrators' blameworthiness. However, this is not to imply that the abuser is absent or free from responsibility. Indeed, in the interviews here, the abuser was an ever-present figure who affected the daily life of the individual. As Dawn says, 'I felt very angry at the time. He probably hasn't thought about it twice and for me it just keeps coming back in various ways.' The following excerpts focus on the role of the perpetrator whose behaviour and actions facilitate both the opportunity to rape and avoid responsibility. The stark contrast between his perception of the situation and the way in which she experiences it is eloquently evidenced.

> It wasn't actually at the party, it happened after and afterwards I took myself off to my room and spent all night convincing myself it hadn't happened. I buried it and then the following day when we were all leaving the house at the same time he said how lovely it had been to meet. (Dawn)

DOI: 10.1057/9781137461728.0005

But then half way through the night he got up and was rifling through the cutlery drawer and I thought that's it. *(Alison: he was going to get a knife.)* I thought that was it. And I er, I think I just lay there motionless absolutely terrified and after about 10 minutes of this rifling through this cutlery drawer he came back with erm, he came back to bed with erm, oh what's it called now? A crème caramel and a spoon. And he sat there eating this, he was just an utter animal. I think at that point I got up to go to the loo and threw up. But it was the most terrifying night of my life. And in the morning, I think he eventually stopped, but in the morning he got up like everything was ok and we got in the car and he dropped us off in the town. (Donna)

(when she was raped by her boyfriend at 15) I was screaming throughout the ordeal but the music (at the party) was very loud and it took a while before anyone heard me and came to the door (of the bedroom) but they obviously couldn't get in (as he had put a wardrobe there). I remember they were banging on the door and he was laughing! I was sick and had wet myself and I was so embarrassed. (Donna)

[bumping into him in town one day] that bad man...c[a]me walking towards me, I couldn't believe, I honestly was so stunned, stunned. And he looked at me and he said 'it's Eliza isn't it?' and I just thought I can't believe after what you did to me, and you're aware of it, that you've got the audacity, audacity.... (Eliza)

When...everything had finished, I put my clothes on and everything...the guy that I had gone back to the, had taken me to the park, he followed me home and I was saying to him, you know, look 'please, please leave me alone' and...he just followed me and I said 'you can't come into my house' and I closed the door and he was really insistent that he was coming into the house, ringing the doorbell, but I lived with eight people at the time.... But that was worse than the actual, than actually what happened...you know,...what happened, he cannot have not thought. He knew I didn't want, I was literally screaming at him to leave me alone. You just think what was that person doing. (Ruby)

Can't believe he didn't hear me screaming (laughs). Maybe I wasn't, maybe I was screaming inside me. I was screaming quietly anyway. I can't believe he couldn't tell from...but I worry that by not having said anything and not having said anything to him or anybody else that he might have gone on and done it again. (Dawn)

The abusers' behaviour is met with incredulity by the women they raped because it seems impossible that the situation could be read any differently. They clearly demonstrated their lack of consent. However women

DOI: 10.1057/9781137461728.0005

express their non-compliance, perpetrators choose to ignore it just as they choose to ignore the significance of their own actions. Donna was certain she was going to be injured or killed when the abuser rifled through the knife drawer, yet he ate as if nothing untoward had happened. And when her boyfriend raped her, he laughed in spite of her obvious screams and embarrassment. Dawn and Ruby exerted as much objection to the behaviour as they could and still the abusers chose to ignore this active non-consent. In pretending not to remember Eliza, her rapist diminishes what happened.

Winkler (2002) argues that in this intimate and power-laden interaction, the perpetrator actively dehumanises her, and these excerpts reveal one of the tactics that facilitates this disregard of her personhood. Sexual violence is not about the misreading of signals, the usual explanation that absolves perpetrators of responsibility (Frith 2009), but involves contrivance. The insidious tactic used here by abusers introduces an element of doubt that immediately causes women to question themselves. In experiencing the situation so differently she wonders whether she misread the situation, especially when she was so completely ignored and disregarded. To be confronted with the person who shared the experience and to have it perceived in such an opposing way begs the question about how others might respond. His contrivance involves tactics, even in those situations that appear spontaneous, which ultimately operate to obscure his accountability. So these excerpts suggest that whilst women acknowledge the presence of the abuser in situations of sexual violence, they were considered no more responsible than observers or facilitators. Indeed, endorsed within culture that denies perpetrator responsibility and silences women from disclosing, such tactics prove successful.

The dehumanisation of women in sexual violence makes allocating responsibility complicated. Such tactics that deflect blame away from those actively involved are reinforced in subsequent interactions, when others trivialise and ignore the rapist's conduct, leaving her in no doubt that she is responsible and that no one will take her seriously. Few mothers supported their daughters, and agencies neglected to act. Donna screamed whilst she was raped by her boyfriend at the age of 16 at a party, but because 'he was laughing' and 'nobody mentioned anything about what happened in the bedroom' she could tell no one about it and felt she was to blame. In highlighting such systematic appropriation and implementation of rape mythology Kelly's (1997a) theory of relative powerlessness is apparent as women are caught in a network of power

DOI: 10.1057/9781137461728.0005

which limits their capacity to act within situations of abuse and in the disclosure of abuse. Yet such a theory also recognises the agency she expends in her expression of non-consent, and the actions she has to take to reduce the severity of the situation and which she later interprets as complicity, within this limiting context. However, accounts from women propose a consideration of the role of others in abuse so that the allocation of responsibility can be adequately understood. The tactics that perpetrators employ (Warner 2007) in conjunction with others' complicity, including collusive practitioners, suggest that responsibility is collectively wrought. To acknowledge this in practice might mean that there are alternatives to self-blame.

Conclusion

Absolving women of responsibility for sexual violence in some feminism and therapy is located in the abdication of their power and control. Whilst rape mythology assigns blame to women who express complicity, this alternative feminist response victimises and ignores often complex power dynamics. Lockwood Harris (2011) highlighted the ways in which women's accounts exist in tension with the prevailing feminist discourse to suggest that the eradication of self-blame as an obligatory part of the healing process undermines the idea that it actually preserves the individual's sense of agency. Instead of accepting their lack of control in sexual violence, women who blame themselves feel that if they had done something differently, they could have had an effect on the situation, to prevent it from happening. Self-blame is not a matter of 'false consciousness', the internalisation of patriarchal indoctrination. Rather, it signifies the struggle to reframe power and control and avoid victimisation. For Brison (2002: 74), women who have experienced sexual violence are 'faced with a choice between regaining control by accepting (at least some) responsibility – and hence blame – for the trauma, or feeling overwhelmed by helplessness.'

Returning to women's accounts, then, the need to engage with responsibility and reconsider agency becomes apparent. Women who have experienced sexual violence are caught up in the constant reiteration of blame that simultaneously denies perpetrator and social responsibility and presumes gender differences which rely on either an idealisation or vilification of women, and mothers in particular. Mardorossian (2014)

DOI: 10.1057/9781137461728.0005

asserts the primacy of sexual violence in the reproduction of gendered power dynamics that are structurally derived rather than biologically determined to suggest that women can occupy and enact masculinity. However, Kelly's (1997a) articulation of relative powerlessness offers a more nuanced theorisation of gender and intersectionality within sexual violence where female complicity in all of its configurations makes sense. This is not to excuse all women of responsibility, as victims of gendered power relations, but to acknowledge the relative power women have in different social situations and in relation to different people. However, sexual violence is an embodied reality of concern not only to women (Mardorossian 2014). In interview extracts women make clear the perpetrators' responsibility and their strategies to dehumanise and deflect blame. Also very clear is our responsibility as individuals within this rape-supportive culture, to notice and act to challenge sexual violence. Otherwise, in our denial of perpetrator and social responsibility, and in our collusion in victim blaming, we effectively leave women who have experienced sexual violence unsafe and with nowhere to go.

DOI: 10.1057/9781137461728.0005

5

Agency

Abstract: *Chapter 5 considers the contemporary feminist articulation of responsibility and female sexual agency in SlutWalk. Two features of neoliberalism, the risk aware and responsible citizen (Anderson and Doherty 2008) and the commodification of experience (Phipps 2015), disrupted SlutWalk's celebration of 'slut' as the essential, active female sexuality. In mainstream media feminism was blamed for sexualising young children. In feminism pro-sex and victim feminists became entrenched and polarised positions. Therefore, returning to women's accounts of sexuality after sexual violence, it is proposed that female sexual agency is neither passive nor free, but nuanced and irreducible to the presence or absence of male sexuality.*

Healicon, Alison. *The Politics of Sexual Violence: Rape, Identity and Feminism.* Basingstoke: Palgrave Macmillan, 2015. DOI: 10.1057/9781137461728.0006.

DOI: 10.1057/9781137461728.0006

it's more like a political thing, sort of maybe moving beyond my personal experience of it or my personal feelings and kind of maybe acting more on a political level rather than on a personal level, like I say for an example,... I am quite open with it now because it was a secret for such a long time and when it all came out ... it was a very freeing experience and I don't ever want to feel like I am like putting it back in a box... even if it's just a case of 'oh well, I'll only bring this out for good friends'. No! It's part of who I am and part of life's experiences, like all sorts of other things, the same way you talk about your family, or ex-boyfriends or where you went to uni, y'know it's just a part of that. But also I got this real kind of political feeling about it sort of being something that I won't be shut up about. And you know not everyone wants to hear it at all and I have had experiences where people are quite like 'oh my god, you're bringing the mood (down)', and I thought no 'I'm not asking you to feel sorry for me, I not asking you to shed a tear' ... 'I'm just telling you that that happened' because it did and maybe if more people said it ...

it wasn't really about me as an individual but about who I am in a social context and I think that's why I feel so strongly, d'you know, about feminism as well because in a way I need to hold onto that in order to ... counter the kind of victim blaming.

(Violet)

Speaking publicly, to another individual or to a wider audience, about experiences of sexual violence is a defiant, validating, political activity that has the potential to transform that which feels shameful, intimate, and personal. Rather than being reduced to, and defined by, incident(s) of abuse, in their articulation, these experiences can be acknowledged as some of the many events that accumulate over a lifetime and which together constitute the whole person. Moreover, also exposed are the tactics and justifications that abusers employ (Warner 2007), to reveal male entitlement as it is channelled through the perpetrator and fuelled by social attitudes which shame and blame the 'victim'. As such, perpetrator-other responsibility becomes visible, thus troubling the criteria by which credibility is assessed. Therefore, in speaking about sexual violence the process of dehumanisation wrought within these specific and abusive

DOI: 10.1057/9781137461728.0006

incident(s) is both highlighted and subverted because personhood is felt to exist beyond the limits of the particular experiences and is contextualised within a culture that tolerates and condones sexual violence. Her character and actions are decentralised, shifting blame and shame away from the individual and onto the perpetrator-other and the politics of the social context in which it takes place and is made meaningful.

Having experiences heard within 'a community of listeners' (Brison 2002), who are empathic, aware, and similarly politically motivated, troubles self-blame, restores credibility, and locates responsibility within the social context. Feminism as a practical and theoretical challenge to male entitlement has provided, and continues to offer, a political community in which experiences of sexual violence are heard and support the possibility for change. However, it is argued in this chapter that the feminist promise of personal and social transformation through the articulation of sexual violence is severely compromised within contemporary neoliberalism, which emphasises penalties for those who ignore risk (Anderson and Doherty 2008) and where personal stories of distress are commoditised and depoliticised (Phipps 2015). Rape Culture minimises and normalises sexual violence through the proliferation of rape mythology and vitriolic victim-blaming, and sits comfortably with neoliberal notions of individual responsibility and risk-aware citizens. This political context is also where feminism takes place and as such it becomes inevitably divided, defensive, and blamed. The consequences are dire for those whose experiences of sexual violence are invalidated in each of these two opposing, yet internally turbulent, processes.

This chapter considers SlutWalk as third-wave feminist activism operating within, and in opposition to, Rape Culture and contemporary neoliberal concerns for risk and blame. SlutWalk attempted to confront directly the issues of credibility and responsibility considered in previous chapters in its central message to reclaim 'slut' and locate responsibility resolutely with the perpetrator in the context of Rape Culture. At its heart, SlutWalk aimed to challenge the rape mythology that renders all women prone to, and responsible for, sexual violence and, in the promotion of a heterogeneous and active female sexuality, encapsulated the politics and possibility of agency and transformation. Once SlutWalk as a political movement is described, Rape Culture as an incarnation of neoliberalism is considered in relation to the public and mainstream media debate at the time, to identify processes that are actively misogynistic. Then, this chapter endeavours to demonstrate how neoliberal concerns for risk

DOI: 10.1057/9781137461728.0006

and commodification of distress (Phipps 2015) compromise SlutWalk as a specific movement within feminism and a particular 'community of listeners' (Brison 2002). In order to elucidate the implications for women who have experienced sexual violence, it is argued that in its attempts to grapple with female sexual agency, SlutWalk potentially perpetuated, rather than challenged or extended our analysis of, neoliberal and patriarchal notions of female sexuality.

SlutWalk

In response to comments by a Toronto police officer in January 2011 that women should avoid dressing like sluts in order to avoid being victimised, the street action phenomenon of 'SlutWalks' spread globally, bringing together a diversity of people to confront attitudes towards rape and reclaim the word 'slut'. The purpose of SlutWalk was to declare the credibility of all women, to challenge the assumption that sexualised clothing causes rape and sexual assault, and to celebrate sexual assertiveness. At the same time SlutWalk called for the accountability of those who perpetrated sexual violence, rather than their 'victims'. SlutWalk UK's message was:

> We want to claim back the word 'slut'...to stop victims being blamed, and blaming themselves. We want to fight sexual stereotypes, and the stereotypes surrounding sexual assault. We're ANGRY about the way...victims of sexual violence are treated and perceived and...want to change this.
>
> This is NOT about hate. We will not tolerate hatred...we want to use the word slut in a positive and empowering way. Sexual assault is not an issue that just concerns women, and...our male allies...can join us on our march. If you're male, female...in between or nothing at all we need you. https://www.facebook.com/slutwalklondonuk/info?tab=page_info

Kruper (2013: np), a commentator on SlutWalk, explains further:

> Slut-shaming is society's attempt to control women's sexuality by shaming them for their sexual actions. Rape Culture, on the other hand, is when society begins to normalise or excuse rape, and is often associated with victim blaming and shaming. SlutWalk attempts to raise awareness of the problems created by slut-shaming and rape culture in hopes of creating a society where these constructs no longer exist.

The prevalence of 'slut' as a justification for sexual violence is directly confronted in the SlutWalk message. In its campaign to expose rape

DOI: 10.1057/9781137461728.0006

mythology and to challenge social attitudes that tolerate rape, SlutWalk focused on two interconnected claims that lie at the heart of credibility assessment and the allocation of responsibility: SlutWalk troubles the notion that prostituted women are perceived of as inherently devoid of credibility and therefore responsible for the sexual violence they experience. It also questions the wider implications for all (girls and) women who are assessed as existing outside of the gendered confines of sexual passivity and restricted sexual expression, since women (and girls) subjected to slut categorisation are similarly rendered incredible and responsible. Reclaiming slut therefore involved asserting the credibility of prostituted women and a celebration of a female sexuality that is obvious and polymorphous rather than constrained and submissive.

It is in the practical application of a post-structural type of feminism that the direct action of SlutWalk expressed these two interconnected claims. SlutWalk attempted to subvert the double standard which grants men a sexual freedom unavailable to women and to trouble credibility assessment through parody and language. The enduring image from SlutWalk is the scantily clad young white woman on whose body slut was written walking with placards proclaiming 'my dress is not a yes'. SlutWalk both appropriated and simultaneously mocked that which is considered 'unacceptable' female attire. Through repetition and positive spin, the category 'slut' was questioned. Just as Butler (1997) suggests in her analysis of hate speech, it is possible to transform the historicity and authority that has congealed around 'slut', in this particular instance, through language itself to dissipate the harm it causes and the power it holds. Such sentiments were articulated in contemporary media reports. For example, in one article at the time Jones (2011: np) exalted the virtues of an approach that involved 'celebrating ... that the word 'slut' is now up-for-grabs because we no longer accept the terms on which it was defined'. For Filar (2011: np), SlutWalk challenged directly slut-shaming, 'by reclaiming the derogatory terms that you use to silence my sexual expression, I dilute your power'. It was suggested through SlutWalk that as long as women maintain control over the creation, promotion, and production of the event, such 'gender manoeuvring' (Finley 2010) in parody and the appropriation of hate speech can transform pariah femininities such as 'slut' into acts of resistance.

Another manifestation of a post-structural type of feminist activism is suggested in SlutWalk's emphasis on diversity and identity rather than material and structural inequalities. SlutWalk promoted itself as diverse

DOI: 10.1057/9781137461728.0006

on the suicide of a 23-year-old woman three days before she was to be tried for perverting the course of justice after the man who raped her began a private prosecution against her in which he accused her of lying about the incident. Even though there was no evidence to suggest she lied to the police in her reporting of the rape, and the Crown Prosecution Service were aware that she was experiencing mental health problems, it appears within the criminal justice system his word was taken more seriously than hers. Additionally, in Smith's (2015) blog entitled 'She Was Gagging for It' cited are the comments of barrister David Osborne who derided the revised prosecution guidelines which place the onus on rape suspects to demonstrate how the complainant consented with 'full capacity and freedom to do so'. Instead Smith (2015: np) suggested he advocates 'a system in which accused men would have a "complete defence" to allegations of rape if the woman was "under the influence"'. Moreover, Osborne (ibid: np) argues,

> In my book, consent is consent, blind drunk or otherwise, and regret after the event cannot make it rape as Ms. Saunders (Director of Public Prosecution who introduced the new guidelines for prosecutors) and Ms. [Harriet] Harman (a renowned feminist MP) seem to be advocating. Save us from the Mssss!

Although Rape Culture is ingrained in all aspects of society, these reports focus on the criminal justice system particularly and demonstrate clearly the dangers involved in the process to incredibility. Women (and girls) are positioned as liars, temptresses, sexually unconstrained and immoral, drunken and slovenly, or mentally unstable, which are contemporaneously held as justifications for disgracing female credibility. Furthermore, the male voice is privileged over their accounts and experiences. Feminist activism via Twitter, Tumblr, and other social media is swift in its response to victim-blaming and yet is simultaneously pilloried, blamed, and accused of irrelevance. Male perpetrators are designated victims of the seductress and 'politically correct' feminism, whilst women are shamed and rendered responsible with fatal consequences. In order to further interrogate slut-shaming and Rape Culture, the responses to SlutWalk within a blog following an article by Germaine Greer (2011) are considered. In so doing, neoliberal concerns for risk and the commodification of experience as they materialise in Rape Culture are explored.

In 'These SlutWalk Women Are Simply Fighting for the Right to Be Dirty' Greer (2011: np) encapsulated the attitude of SlutWalk in

DOI: 10.1057/9781137461728.0006

connecting the original use of the word 'slut', as a dirty or slovenly person, to the more gender-specific contemporary definition, a woman of loose morals or who is sexually promiscuous:

> No house is ever clean enough, no matter how many hours its resident woman spends spraying and wiping...disinfecting and deodorising. Women's bodies can never be washed...enough to be entirely free of dirt; they must be depilated and deodorised...When it comes to sex, women are as dirty as the next man, but they don't have the same right to act out their fantasies. If they're to be liberated, women have to demand the right to be dirty. By declaring themselves sluts, they lay down the Cillit Bang and take up the instruments of pleasure.

Greer suggests that in taking on the mantle of slut, SlutWalking women choose to disregard social convention and declare themselves liberated from the constraints on female sexual agency, thereby eradicating slut shame specifically and generally. In particular, SlutWalk legitimates prostitution as sex work devoid of social stigma, and reconsiders more generically slut as a positive and active sexuality. Moreover, in choosing to rid themselves of such constraints SlutWalking women are free to expose, and celebrate, an inherent and essential 'dirty-ness'. An approach that suggests, in their declaration of sexual freedom, women can simply walk away from gendered oppression is problematic and discussed later in relation to the feminist debate. However, in the wider public domain this SlutWalk message was missed and misappropriated. Within mainstream media, the choice of women to engage more actively with their individual sexual identity and expression metamorphosed into a risky and potentially hazardous personal decision. This choice was also diverted into debates about sexualisation. Western women, veil-wearing Muslim women, and children were set in opposition to each other in a commoditisation of experience.

These extracts have been taken (and anonymised) from a publicly available blog following Greer's article on 13 May 2011 to demonstrate the typical tropes employed in media discussion of SlutWalk at the time. The regularly repeated analogy in the blog was that in order not to have our possessions stolen it is our responsibility to keep them secure.

> No one has said...rape and nicking a car are in the same moral category...there are parallels in how people can take measures that reduce or increase the likelihood of either crime happening without reducing the severity of the crime in the eyes of the law if those precautions are not taken. One of the problems...is that feminists...set things up so that it is

DOI: 10.1057/9781137461728.0006

impossible to say anything... except pat clichés about how bad rape is... what advice do you think it IS ok to give women about how to protect themselves from sexual attack? (danielGB85)

Why do women need to take such measures... ask... yourself that? Or challenge... the notions that give rise to some men feeling they can take whatever they... please like... rutting stags because a woman is 'asking for it'? Never mind the awfulness of being forced off a street... you would far sooner... call me a liar than deal with the very raw issues rape victims face... faced with a non-feminist challenging the hideously ugly inhuman commentary from men... the knee jerk reaction is to call that person a liar... Rape isn't a lie.... It's a real and nasty issue a good number of women such as myself and our families deal with dignity... ask yourself what... YOU can do to challenge the men who feel they can rape with impunity when they see women they are attracted to?... Instead of forcing women to be continually on their guard... (Camdenistar)

There are some men in the world who will commit rape. This is a facet of the human race. Just as some women will neglect their children... the problem is never going to go away. So... people need to... protect themselves... not put themselves at increased risk in order to make feminists feel better. (danielGB85)

... (so) rape is... just a crime and a threat to be wholly reduced by... women. For women it involves compromising... freedoms and the result of a rape can be... more debilitating than the effects of other crime. The problem is... not going to go away by insisting women compromise... freedoms and that we somehow invite rape. The... issue is wholly skewed... where women... need to take responsibility to avoid rape and men... don't. (Camdenistar)

... I suggest you get some therapy. You seem totally neurotic... (eduke)

Wear whatever... you like .... But... if you hide your face, people will be suspicious of you, and if you dress like a 'slut', you are more likely to draw the eye of predators. Do either.... But don't whine about the inevitable responses to your choice. (danielGB85)

If you dress like a hooker, don't be surprised if people treat you like one. (a.nother)

The continual trivialisation of sexual violence by the male protagonists is striking and so entrenched that no alternative understanding appears possible. Not only is it a 'cliché about how bad rape is' and a crime comparable to theft, but the woman, who has named her experience in the blog, is eventually silenced as neurotic. Despite declaring herself a non-feminist and having clearly articulated problems inherent to the biological determinism of their argument, in suggesting she requires

DOI: 10.1057/9781137461728.0006

'therapy' the male adversaries tactically obliterate her credibility and minimise sexual violence generally. The male response presumes madness, which operates to invalidate her experiences, and therefore the experiences of others. As a consequence, her (and any other) political viewpoint based on these experiences is easily disregarded. It has become inconceivable that within 'madness' there is credibility. Moreover, central to Rape Culture in its trivialisation of sexual violence is the neoliberal concern for responsible choice, also evident in this conversation. The male response additionally assumes that in choosing to speak from her experience she has exposed her already 'discreditable' positioning and in naming her experience in this particular domain she has again chosen to make herself vulnerable. In their minds, because of the choices she has made, she is fair game. This association of neoliberal choice, credibility, and responsibility is evident in three key themes apparent in this extract and in discussions on sexual violence in mainstream media.

The first theme, evident within this extract, involves this location of responsibility for sexual violence solely with the woman because she 'chose' to put herself in danger. Anderson and Doherty (2008) suggest that neoliberalism relies on the reflexive, risk aware, and self-regulating subject. Choice, therefore, is an effect of the autonomous and responsible citizen assessing and avoiding risky situations. It is assumed that 'reasonable' women would make themselves hazard aware and take the necessary precautions to keep safe. In the extract, the two men assert that women know the risks and as such the choice is clear: to be responsible and conventional, or to 'dress like a slut', lose credibility, and suffer the consequences without 'whining'. It is incomprehensible in this conversation that inhabiting the proscriptive confines of female sexuality is no guarantee of safety for women either. Rather, victimisation signifies a reckless individual (that is, someone who was drunk, wore a short skirt, was 'unladylike', involved in sex work, etc.) who 'chooses' to expose themselves to dangers in society and of a failure to make responsible adjustments. Within neoliberalism and Rape Culture, a victim is both culpable and blameworthy.

Anderson and Doherty (2008) also identify another three elements of neoliberal risk taking that are relevant to this discussion here and to the later debate on SlutWalk. They suggest that within neoliberalism the self-sufficient individual has no need to rely on the state for support or protection as it is their responsibility to take care of themselves. Translated into the sexual violence field, Warner (2003) claims, a 'recovered' subject

DOI: 10.1057/9781137461728.0006

is one who is manageable and predictable and no longer a 'nuisance' to others or public services. In the extract, this element of neoliberalism is revealed in the assertion that the woman should 'get some therapy'. In this statement two mutually exclusive assumptions are conjoined to blame her. Not only have they previously suggested she is lying or exaggerating, but this statement presumes a self-regulating and self-improving citizen, responsible for her own recovery, thus rendering possible some 'damage' that they originally disclaim. However, the apparent devolution of power in the form of responsibility to the individual away from the dissociated and shrunken state is a smokescreen that has much wider implications. It forecloses an alternative perspective, that sexual violence is the responsibility of the perpetrator-other within the specific cultural context. In this dissociation, the individual's connection to collective community support is severely restricted, and in the obfuscation of social responsibility, opportunities for proper protection and justice are also curtailed. In this cultural climate it becomes easier to implicate women in their responsibility for sexual violence and recovery and more justifiable to withdraw support from unrecovered or incredible 'victims'.

Anderson and Doherty suggest that this laissez-faire language of neoliberal capitalism, which equates the global free market with growth, security, and prosperity, seeps into the social sphere. In the social market place, individuals negotiate and compete with others in order to secure and protect their various interests. As the woman in the extract suggests, sexual violence is a 'compromise in freedoms' as sexual encounters are articulated in terms of reciprocal transactions of losses and gains. Furthermore, unrecovered and incredible 'victims' are positioned as a drain on valuable resources. However, Anderson and Doherty argue that this neoliberal conception of human interaction as a mutually beneficial exchange presupposes that differences and inequalities are matters of mere personal choice. For example, choosing to express sexuality through appearance, or choosing to engage in sex work, or choosing to consume alcohol all suggest that such sexual negotiations are based on positions of preference and reciprocity. As such, sexual violence is reduced to problematic communication and mixed messages as any analysis of gendered power relations, and intersectional inequality is precluded.

The second theme evident in this extract, and pertinent to the later SlutWalk discussion, concerns the commodification of experience (Phipps 2015). Within the framework of neoliberalism – which Phipps

(2015: np) claims 'individualises, interiorises, and neutralises' – personal experience becomes co-opted, diverted, and transformed to fit the political agenda of those who make use of the particular narratives. Furthermore, in order to fulfil such ideological and often opposing demands, lived realities are 'flattened out', reducing complex experiences to simple, homogenised, and polarised arguments. The ramifications are twofold: personal experience is de-humanised and corrupted, and the space in between for debate, which holds ambivalence and explores nuance, is closed. In this particular extract the politics of sexual violence were conflated with issues of choice and co-opted into wider public debates of the time around sexualisation and the hijab as a symbol of oppression. As one of the men opines:

> Wear whatever ... you like .... But ... if you hide your face, people will be suspicious of you, and if you dress like a 'slut', you are more likely to draw the eye of predators. Do either .... But don't whine about the inevitable responses to your choice.

Responsibility and choice continue to dominate in this statement. Yet choosing to 'dress like a slut' is now aligned with choosing to 'hide your face'. Either way, choosing to conceal or reveal the female body incurs 'inevitable responses'. In this extract there is an underlying (and misguided) warning that women should choose responsibly to tread the narrow path of safe respectability, between totally covering and exposing the body, or suffer the consequences. The lived realities and the political challenges that SlutWalk and wearing the veil encompass are simplified and reduced to a choice that sustains suspicion and violence. The commodification of these particular experiences was also found in other broadsheets. Muslim women and SlutWalkers were not only set against each other but also alongside other experiences, with 'inevitable responses' articulated.

For example, in one Observer article (McVeigh 2011) commentators described SlutWalkers as liberated, political, and essentially Westernised, in contrast to the 'oppressed, veiled Muslim woman' (Pedwell 2011: 189). Although it was acknowledged that choice of attire is politically motivated in both situations, Western women were positioned with agency in their capacity to challenge inequality. Whilst the 'inevitable responses' for veiled women are therefore pity or suspicion, the commentators' response to SlutWalkers was to extend the bounds of female responsibility to incorporate the potential impact that such displays of sexuality

DOI: 10.1057/9781137461728.0006

had on younger women. The needs of adult SlutWalkers to assert and celebrate their sexuality in order to confront slut-shaming were not only positioned in relation to 'oppressed Muslim women' but also as potentially harmful to children. As one of the female commentators in McVeigh's (2011: np) article suggests:

> while I found the way the [Toronto] policeman expressed himself completely inappropriate ... I do wonder about a lot of the fashion now, with young girls ... dressing very provocatively ... perhaps they don't realise the subliminal message they send out. So there is an interpretation ... more sympathetic to his view ... that ... women can be making themselves vulnerable, particularly young girls. Our very sexualised society puts pressure on young girls.... If they gave it more thought they wouldn't feel comfortable with what they're saying about themselves.

The political message of SlutWalk to recognise the responsibility of the perpetrator was missed as it became diverted into contemporary concerns about the sexualisation of young people (Popadopoulos 2010). These cultural fears, that young girls may not have the maturity to understand the possible consequences of such sexual expression and indeed may be psychologically damaged by social pressures to behave and appear sexualised, were privileged over perpetrator-other responsibility. The obvious sexual expression of SlutWalkers was evidence of their participation in this possible corruption of young girls. In this debate, the representations of the veiled Muslim woman, the slut, or the sexualised child became entrenched positions. Experiences were dehumanised and contorted to fit the political agenda of the speaker. Women's lives were extricated from the complex realities of intersecting inequalities, and agency was defined only in relation to individual responsibility within the confines of a choice that suggests safety for women is possible. Such commodification of experience facilitates the denial of perpetrator and social responsibility for sexual violence and as Phipps (2015) suggests, minimises opportunities to fully engage, emotionally and practically, with different experiences.

SlutWalk was founded on creating opportunities to learn from the diversity of experiences of those involved. Yet, the third identifiable theme articulated in the original excerpt and within Rape Culture is feminism as an outmoded, misguided, and corrupting influence. Feminism was blamed for restricting the debate, for setting 'things up so that it is impossible to say anything'. SlutWalk was also accused of duping other women because 'people need to ... protect themselves ... not put

DOI: 10.1057/9781137461728.0006

themselves at increased risk in order to make feminists feel better'. In the sexualisation debate, feminists risked being positioned as lacking moral integrity for suggesting that young people's negotiation of sexualisation is 'complex' (Ringrose 2011). SlutWalk demonstrates that the political motivation to make a difference in specific aspects of women's lives continues to be significant. The wider political impetus to challenge and eradicate rape-supportive infrastructure through SlutWalk, however, was misrepresented and instead reduced to the sole need of women and girls to have information to help make responsible choices to keep themselves safe. In mainstream media feminism is sidelined, deemed irrelevant in our equality (McRobbie 2009) and dangerous. It is apparent in these excerpts that credibility and responsibility are only ever conventionally articulated and that the possibility of reclaiming 'slut' as a viable and credible category is extremely remote.

Feminist debate

Analysis of the mainstream media debate revealed the reproduction of rape mythology and the operation of neoliberal processes of individualism and compartmentalisation which absented perpetrator-other responsibility and trivialised the voices of women who have experienced sexual violence. Yet within feminism, 'slut' as a viable category for reclamation was also contested. At the heart of this feminist debate was a theoretical and practical engagement with what it means to be a woman, and in a process of commodification of experience, SlutWalk became further entrenched in internal oppositional politics. Whilst in the mainstream, SlutWalk's celebration of inherent sluttiness further confirmed conventional justifications for sexual violence, for Attwood (2007: 245), '[s]truggles over sluttiness have become part of a struggle over feminism itself'. However, the problem with defining female sexuality as inherently slutty is twofold. This position doesn't necessarily challenge underlying structural oppression and rape-supportive infrastructure in which slut-shaming and responsibility are inextricably linked. Also, such debates do not necessarily progress an articulation of female sexual agency, but rather the reformulation of male sexuality. So in a return to the voices of women who have experienced sexual violence, in a process of 'unthinking',[1] this section also considers some of the issues encountered in directly transposing the language of male sexuality onto female sexuality.

DOI: 10.1057/9781137461728.0006

It has already been suggested that SlutWalk, as a practical engagement with post-structural feminism, confronted slut-shaming through language and a celebration of diversity. The following excerpts, taken from a variety of sources, exemplify the framing of this particular story within the feminist debate:

> Unlike protests... by mainstream... women's organisations, which are carefully planned... SlutWalks have cropped up organically... fuelled by raw emotional and political energy of young women... the success of SlutWalks does herald a new day in feminist organising... women's anger begins online but takes to the street... a local step makes global waves... that will have lasting effects on the movement. (Valenti 2011: np)

> the crowd identified with sex workers. There was such empathy when two women from the English Collective of Prostitutes spoke that my first thought was that this was a sex worker audience... I then realised that the line between women who turn tricks and women who don't was almost invisible... it was not a moral divide, but one of chance and choice... we were marching because it wasn't anyone's business what any of us did with our bodies... transgender, lesbian, straight and bisexual women. We were not merely marching together; we were one, claiming not equality but mutual respect for individuality. Establishing your right establishes and safeguards mine. (James 2011: np)

> I don't think this is a protest about identity, I think it's a protest about language. (Jones 2011: np)

> The organisers claim that celebrating the word 'slut', and promoting sluttishness... will help women achieve... autonomy over their sexuality. But... 'reclaiming' the word slut fails to address the real issue... slut is so deeply rooted in the patriarchal 'madonna/whore' view of women's sexuality that it is beyond redemption.... Encouraging women to be even more 'sluttish' will not change this ugly reality... the organisers of the SlutWalk might think that proudly calling themselves 'sluts' is a way to empower women, they are in fact making life harder for girls... trying to navigate their way through the tricky terrain of adolescence. Women need to take to the streets – but not for the right to be called 'slut'. (Dines and Murphy 2011: np)

> for a prostituted girl or woman... enslaved in the sex trade, the word 'slut' could mean abuse, sexual torture, terror and exploitation. For many, to be a 'slut'... means to hang between life and death. Would these women really want to reclaim the word 'slut' when that is what it means to them? (blog response to Jones 2011: np)

> is undressing the best way to protest against rape?' (Gold 2011: np)

DOI: 10.1057/9781137461728.0006

> I completely understand the motivation behind SlutWalk…I'm simply not personally comfortable marching…under the banner 'slut'. It's not how I define myself…(or)…how I want other people to view me. The use of the word has brought global media attention to…victim blaming, which is fantastic, and…makes complete sense in the context…so I'm not going to deny it was a great idea. I just don't want to go on a march myself, and…their [sic] are other feminists who feel the same. It's not that we don't 'get it', it's that slutwalking isn't an approach that we…favour, for a whole variety of reasons. (Woodhouse 2011: np)

Inclusion, fun, and individualism are the three characteristics of third-wave feminism outlined by Budgeon (2011) that are apparent in the ethics, delivery, and content of SlutWalk. Instigated by young women, proponents celebrated SlutWalk as inclusive of diversity with particular emphasis on the participation of black and working-class women, sex workers, male feminists, and people identifying as transgender. SlutWalk rejected 'victim' feminism that denied female agency and positioned all women as casualties of an oppressive patriarchy, in favour of fun and sexy empowerment with attitude, where women are agents in control of their (sexual) life. The politics of SlutWalk was not collective action but a collection of politically divergent people brought together, as Budgeon (2011: 283) suggests, 'to define their personal relationship to feminism in ways that make sense to them as individuals'. Passionately and organically disseminated, the SlutWalk message was not about 'equality but mutual respect for individuality', nor was it 'a protest about identity' but 'language'. Content concerned the legitimation of sex work and reduction of stigma in order to assert a polymorphous, active female sexuality. The delivery and content of the SlutWalk message was asserted to indicate a distinction from, and an opposition to, the feminism of the 1970s and 1980s which was articulated as exclusionary, essentialist, and hard-line.

SlutWalk distanced itself from earlier incarnations of feminism just as feminist critics questioned an approach that both relied on the exposure of women's bodies (was 'undressing the best way to protest against rape?') and disregarded fundamental structural and institutional inequalities, to further establish an oppositional politics. For Walia (2011: np; and Islam 2011) SlutWalk acknowledged 'slut' as a category that 'disproportionately impacts women of colour and poor women to reinforce their status as inherently dirty…second-class…more rape-able', but it was unable to respond to the accusation that reclaiming 'slut' is easier for some white women. The main controversy within the feminist debate, however, inevitably concentrated on the prostituted woman. Third-wave SlutWalk discourse emphasised choice, pleasure, and validation of experiences of women involved in pornography and prostitution. Conversely, critics focused on accounts that highlighted the harm of both. For example, Coy (2009: 201) suggests that even without violence and coercion, selling sex is characterised 'by a sense of intrusion, dissociation and (dis)embodiment'. SlutWalk proponents advocated for the decriminalisation and the consequent legitimation of sex work in order to secure women's rights and control over their working environment thereby eliminating stigma considered the only barrier to validation. Whereas feminist critics of SlutWalk focused on removing the demand for prostitution since structural inequalities render prostitution dangerous for the majority of women involved. In their assertion of an active female sexuality, SlutWalkers demanded choice to participate in pornography and sex work in defiance of the perceived anti-sex view that prostitution is a process of re-victimisation. Although at the heart of the debate is the recognition that the female body matters, and responsibility for sexual violence lies with the perpetrator-other, positions became entrenched. The prostituted woman, as the embodiment of society's censure and victim-blaming, both susceptible to sexual violence and responsible for it, was contested territory in a battle to define women's sexuality and ultimately feminism itself.

The infiltration of neoliberal concerns for individualism and the commodification of experience is clearly apparent in this feminist debate. Both elements are detrimental to the progression of a nuanced and contrary praxis necessary to challenge the predominance of Rape Culture. SlutWalk's sexually autonomous female agent accepts and enjoys an inherent sluttiness and as such her sexuality, and intimate encounters, become unencumbered by social constraints. She is free to make informed choices and to consent in sexual relations based on a negotiation and mutual exchange of personal interest. However, this neoliberal risk-aware individual, responsible only to herself, may be able to celebrate a previously denied sexuality, but it depends on an equality that does not exist and a negation of power that saturates each social situation. Moreover, sluttiness, as an expression of sexual difference, in actuality encapsulates an exaggerated heteronormative sexuality which absolutely reproduces social censure and processes to credibility. The very rules sluttiness attempts to displace are further ensconced as these demonstrations of female sexuality incite further social criticism.

DOI: 10.1057/9781137461728.0006

The individualism of SlutWalk was confronted in critical feminist responses because it ignored structural inequalities and depoliticised feminism as collective action. Unfortunately, this argumentation was absorbed into the entrenched positioning that relied on the opposition of second- and third-wave feminism, foreclosing dialogue and consideration of continuities and coherence. Drawing on Phipps' (2015) notion of commodification of experience, particular and 'flattened out' experiences were set against each other and the surrounding politics ignored. In their articulation of 'slut', prostituted women were either dupes and/or victims of patriarchy or liberated and self-possessed sex radicals. There was no space in which to narrate or recognise the subtlety of contradictory experience. 'In this politics of positionality', Phipps (2015: np) argues, 'experiences are always already marked by ideology and the first question we ask (consciously or not) when someone shares their experience is, "whose side are you on?"' The oppositional politics evidenced in SlutWalk is fundamentally problematic for both individual identity and the identity of feminism. 'Them and us' situations polarise and reduce experience and, in a process of abjection (Butler 2004), eradicate the possibility of a more intricate and alternative subjectivity. Simultaneously, within feminism the space to discuss commonalities and complexity is reduced whilst in the public domain both sides of the feminist argument are discredited as feminism is portrayed as either dangerous in its proscription of free sexuality, or moralistic in its policing of 'slut'. Internal feminist debates are not publicly acknowledged and therefore the possibility of nuance is lost, as feminism is perceived as obsolete.

SlutWalk attempted to trouble generic and feminist representations of female sexuality as inevitably passive. Given the scale of sexual violence and the proliferation of rape-supportive presumptions and practices, it is expedient to both consider female sexuality as relational and subordinate, and to demand to signify it differently. Rather than subscribe to the oppositional politics that emerged from the neoliberalism of SlutWalk, which asserted either a passive or a male-oriented female sexuality, it is perhaps strategic instead to recognise the complexity of sexual agency that is apparent within women's accounts. It has been previously argued that rape is intimately sexualised and experienced as the destruction of (sexual) identity. Moreover, women feel complicit if they have instigated or responded biologically to sexual violence. Indeed any situation where the individual's sexuality is manipulated for perpetrator gain causes confusion and reveals inherent power dynamics. Therefore, in their articulation of

DOI: 10.1057/9781137461728.0006

the destruction of sexuality in violence, in these accounts, women offer a starting point from which to 'unthink' female sexual agency that is neither passive nor free, but nuanced and irreducible to the presence or absence of male sexuality. Ultimately these extracts reveal the need to problematise cultural presumptions that both subsume female sexuality to managing trauma or to responsibility for her own and male sexual behaviour.

And I felt quite promiscuous after [being raped].... But then I built up a relationship with a bloke who, it was more a friendship, who helped me really. *(Alison: How?)* I don't know, just being there really.... I'd not seen him for about 18 months and I knocked on his door once and it was after I had reported [the rapist to the police].... Been for a bottle of wine at [my friend's] and when I come home I opened another one... I would be drunk then.... And he was so shocked to see me. Basically I wanted him to sleep with me but I didn't want sex. I don't know what I wanted. I wanted to feel worse. And he was very good. I mean I didn't say 'I want to sleep with you', but I was obviously very vulnerable and he respected my vulnerability really... he didn't take advantage of it. (Eliza)

But I do think the effects are that I read into things too much now... I become an emotional... caretaker for people.... Not because I'm a good person... I feel because of my knowledge I can protect. Well, no I can't. You protect yourself. (Eliza)

My first husband was very, very supportive, very.... In fact I was going out with him for quite a long time before we had physical contact and he was so patient and he knew why and I always found [sex] painful, physically painful... and I never made the link but it always brought me to tears. And... it's only recently that I've made that link. That it saddened and distressed me so much the actual act and disgusted me that it brought me to tears. And my husband was like 'what is wrong?' and I didn't know, it just happens. But that stopped after the counselling. Just like that. It was not something that I thought I had any control over. (Donna)

I hated men basically, I hated them. I just saw each and every one of them as predators, even my husband when I married him. It's like if he did certain things like, if he tried to have sex with me in the middle of the night it disgusted me, it horrified me and it would take me back. (Donna)

maybe one effect of the trauma is... you sort of sexualise other people and you feel you can only get love through sex, or you can get something like affirmation or any good feelings through sex. What you really want is a friendship. (Elaine)

The perpetrator's colonisation of her embodied self precipitates a dispute over the physical, psychological, and sexual ownership of her mind and

DOI: 10.1057/9781137461728.0006

body. Sex after sexual violence, therefore, is understandably problematic in its potential to activate physical and emotional pain. SlutWalk's insistence on embracing and liberating a free and polymorphous sexuality is, therefore, not reflected in these accounts. Neither is the passive and victimised sexuality of SlutWalk critics. Instead women articulate the need to test, evaluate, and to challenge previously held and socially constructed beliefs about a female sexuality that is constrained within gendered power relations. There is much to consider within these frank and emotive extracts, but highlighted here are two main areas of concern that demonstrate nuance and complexity, to supplement the 'flattened out' and opposing experiences proffered in the SlutWalk debate. Firstly, sexual violence causes her, and others (friends, partners, professionals, etc.) to critically reinterpret her sexuality and sexual expression, and secondly, this re-evaluation, which focuses on women's sexual behaviour, detracts critical attention away from male sexuality as *the* explanatory framework.

Critical re-evaluation of her sexuality prompts a number of fearful possibilities particularly related to her sexuality, including the fear of vulnerability, fear of perpetual victimhood, and fear of difference. Articulated in the excerpts is a vulnerability that is both naive, propelling her into unsafe predicaments, and knowing, since it is presumed that experiential knowledge of dehumanisation assists her to identify oppressive situations and behaviours that are best avoided. However, whether naive or knowledgeable, for Mardorossian (2014) vulnerability is inextricably linked to responsibility within contemporary 'rape victim' identity as she is held responsible for managing her vulnerability before and after the event(s). As such she may blame herself not only in light of an unfavourable reinterpretation of her previous 'negligence' but also for making insufficient use of her experiential knowledge to protect her present self and others. Moreover, Reavey (2003) suggests that female sexuality is measured in relation to abuse and the damage it produces so that any subsequent sexual relationships, whether problematic or not, are defined only in relation to the incidences of abuse. Participation and enjoyment of penetrative heterosex is considered evidence of progress, of her taking responsibility to repair her 'damaged' sexuality. Reavey (2003) argues that women's sexuality is monitored in terms of the reiteration of, or recovery from, a perpetual victimhood. Thus affirming her difference from 'normal' women who are neither alienated from their sexuality nor privy to the circumstantial knowledge of vulnerability. However, as Reavey suggests, ignored are the gendered power relations apparent in all women's lives.

DOI: 10.1057/9781137461728.0006

The excerpts expose the spotlighting of female sexuality as the arbiter of sexual responsibility which justifies the need for its continual scrutiny and evaluation. As progress is assessed in relation to her sexual encounters, her responsibility for male sexuality becomes apparent. For example, Eliza and Donna saw all men as sexually predatory; therefore, even 'supportive' men who acknowledged their vulnerability and refrained from sex required testing. This presumption of female responsibility that incongruently requires the monitoring of her sexuality rather than his obscures the significance of male sexuality as *the* filter through which all sexuality is known. Amara (2015) draws upon her own and other women's experience of sexuality after sexual violence to suggest that it is from the perpetrator's perspective that she understands her own embodied self. For example, in her article, Amara (2015: np) cites one woman who fears catching sight of her body because it will 'be like looking through the eyes of [her] rapist. [Her] body is the image he must have seen. [She doesn't] want to look through his eyes ... [she] wants [her] body back.' The struggle to reclaim her body is more than the desire for situated ownership, but an imperative to define herself independently from him, to know herself not through the male gaze or from the male perspective, but on her own terms. Scrutiny of female sexuality is both a distraction from the significance of male sexuality and a necessity in order to review and renew connection to her body and sex. It is both an imposition of gendered norms and a challenge to them.

If male sexual agency is an imposition that obliterates alternative descriptors so that female sexuality is defined only as an imitation of male sexuality, then consideration of sexuality within and after sexual violence is significant. The process of reclaiming her body, self, and sexuality in the aftermath of such destruction could be mirrored theoretically in order to define female sexuality on our own terms. These accounts suggest that female sexuality is not an appropriation of male sexual behaviour and attitudes as proposed in SlutWalk. Nor is female sexuality the moderate, temperate, or sensible antithesis of the male agency articulated in the public domain either. However, just as women here suggest, given the pervasiveness of this male perspective, possible alternatives are limited.

Conclusion

Speaking out loud experiences of sexual violence is an agentic and political act. It exposes secrets, identifies commonalities that alleviate stigma,

DOI: 10.1057/9781137461728.0006

and names operations of oppression. In contemporary Western neoliberalism that reifies the autonomous, proactive, and responsible citizen, collective naming of experience and resistance to slut-shaming on such a global scale as that of SlutWalk demonstrates an unprecedented demand for feminism. However, the existence of 'slut' as a misogynist category in itself was not properly articulated (Murphy 2012). Instead SlutWalk assumed elements of neoliberalism that further entrenched political divisions and left the general public unaffected by a feminism that was perceived as at best irrelevant and at worst dangerous. It also promoted a controversial exposition of female sexuality as polymorphous, active, and unfettered by traditional gendered constraints that denied the existence of structural inequalities and left unchallenged the predominantly masculine template that proscribes sexuality. Although SlutWalk asserted multiplicity, it simply transposed male sexuality onto women.

In consideration of women's accounts of sexuality after sexual violence, it becomes apparent that such a response is problematic. If rape, as Mardorossian (2014) suggests, is a fundamental incarnation of the hegemonic masculine will to dominate that necessitates the subjugation of the feminised other, then examination of rape exposes sexuality that is constituted in oppression. That is, sexual violence does not reveal the essence of heterosexuality, nor does it suggest an extreme and unusual manifestation of masculinity because it is not contingent on biologically sexed bodies. Rape defines sexual relations and sexuality particularly because it is the enactment and reproduction of structural inequalities through the will to dominate. Although the sexuality of SlutWalk highlights societal double standards where normalised sexual behaviour considered acceptable in men is condemned in women. In its insistence on the appropriation of male sexuality as the template of all sexuality, it actually and inadvertently reinforces the categorising duality of female passivity and male agency it attempts to dispel, thereby perpetuating the very structural inequalities that legitimise the will to dominate. No alternative definition of female sexuality is offered here, but rather an understanding of sexuality that incorporates nuance and complexity as it is reconstructed after sexual violence.

Note

1 Thank you to Lyra for suggesting this term.

DOI: 10.1057/9781137461728.0006

6
Practice

Abstract: *The concluding chapter attends to the demands of feminist research to improve practice response. In order to assess the study's contribution, therefore, a summary of the concerns highlighted within women's accounts is provided, as they challenge the categorisation and essentialism of victim identity, and expose secondary harm that blames the violated woman and denies social responsibility. Representing rape carefully (Gay 2014) raises issues for practice and highlights the limitations of the research. Good practice responses are summarised in recommendations.*

Healicon, Alison. *The Politics of Sexual Violence: Rape, Identity and Feminism.* Basingstoke: Palgrave Macmillan, 2015. DOI: 10.1057/9781137461728.0007.

> I had nowhere to turn, the bad [children's] homes were abusive. Staff didn't give a shit anyway.
>
> (Amy)
>
> There's nothing worse when people are grasping for support when somebody sits on the fence. Get off the fence and join them or don't bloody bother.
>
> (Eliza)
>
> I care passionately about people being able to live life, not being constricted by this crap. I think that is the ultimate success of the abuser…. It isn't what they did at the time, it's what they make us stop achieving.
>
> (Caitlin)
>
> Wow. This is scary stuff. Am I a self-disciplining, recovered woman? Is that how I position myself not to be feared/ rejected/ ostracised/ looked down on? Are my attempts of liberation and empowerment in fact leading to greater subjugation and oppression?
>
> (Violet)

In an attempt to write sexual violence 'carefully' (Gay 2014), without trivialising or sensationalising, and with a passion for precision and dissemination, this book detailed the experiences and priorities of 12 women who have been raped. Focussing particularly on their articulation of the reality of rape and the limits to self-presentation, these more rounded and less 'flattened out' (Phipps 2015) accounts offered nuance and complexity. In doing so, the book exposed and challenged the polarisation implicated in processes of compartmentalisation, which ranks experiences such as stranger and date rape, and categorisation, where identity is assessed for credibility and innocence, or responsibility and deficiency. In accordance with the wishes of the women who participated, this book theorises the possibility of living beyond, and in contradiction to, the socially ascribed labels implicit within the harm story of abuse (O'Dell 2003), which establishes the inevitable damage of the traumatised yet stigmatised 'rape victim', or the victim-blaming misogyny of rape mythology. The research aims were, therefore, to trouble processes of compartmentalisation and categorisation (Mardorossian 2014) contained within psychological and public discourse, in order to

DOI: 10.1057/9781137461728.0007

facilitate a more faithful account of sexual violence and to situate blame and responsibility with the perpetrator-other.

For women who have experienced sexual violence, it is important to acknowledge and appreciate trauma, the particularities of terminology and therapeutic strategies that help describe and manage emotional distress, and opportunities to access a range of support including counselling. However, this book does not pursue a therapeutic approach, it does not prescribe a route to recovery, nor does it offer practical coping techniques or exercises. Indeed, the predominance and prioritisation of a psychological response is contested as a product of a therapy culture (Furedi 2004) that surveils and delimits self-expression and identity. So how is this book useful, then? In taking seriously women's accounts, it confirms the necessity of an alternative and feminist consideration of sexual violence that does not differentiate between experiences, or assess for credibility or harm. It situates the experience and representation of rape, and the behaviour and responsibility of the perpetrator, within the context of contemporary but persistent and entrenched power dynamics and intersectional inequalities. This book engages with feminism and philosophy to consider subjectivity as neither biologically determined or free, but complicit and resistant, articulating theoretically the possibility of agency or transformation, which are significant themes in women's accounts. So although this book does not offer practical strategies and solutions, it is pragmatic in its analysis of a politics of transformation, as it is necessarily narrated in the extracts above.

Kelly (1988: 73) suggested feminist research that focuses particularly on gendered violence requires 'a commitment which includes not condoning abuse explicitly or implicitly, seeing the purpose…as increasing understanding in order that more appropriate responses can be developed, and wanting to contribute to a long term goal of ending violence in the lives of women and children'. Applying theory to practice in order to make a difference in women's lives was the primary motivation for seeking publication and precipitated the participation of women into this study. Given the extent of Rape Culture and the proliferation of the harm story, women who have experienced sexual violence may find clarity in the presentation of narratives that communicate missing nuance to plug some of the gaps created in processes of compartmentalisation and categorisation. However, in spite of good intentions, it is impossible to measure impact or contribution to ending violence. The responsibilities of the research(er) therefore are more tangibly evaluated here in relation

DOI: 10.1057/9781137461728.0007

to the possibility of developing practice responses and avoiding excuses for male-perpetrated violence against women and girls. There are four main areas in which this research has contributed to knowledge. It has provided: nuances in experience that suggest the contemporary category of 'rape victim' is both accepted and rejected, critique of the essentialism of the gendering of the 'rape victim', details of secondary harm, and details of social responsibility. These themes are discussed to summarise the concerns of women who have experienced sexual violence as they have been articulated within this research. Further practical implications are identified within a consideration of the limitations of the study and then recommendations for practice are collated and suggested.

Contribution to knowledge

It has been argued that sexual violence destroys the self (Winkler 2002) which, in therapeutic and psychological literature, devastates the individual's relationship with her body and with the community. Without denying the possibility, or the effects, of trauma, this research opposed the pathologisation of subjectivity in order to facilitate capacity for individual and social change. The traumatised and dissociated self, arguably indicative of psychological damage, was reformulated to suggest a potentially transformative, fluid, and multiple subjectivity that is dependent upon, and constituted within, the intra-actions of bodies, social spaces, structures, and language. Other studies similarly advocate multiplicity and fluidity, in order to avoid pathologisation and promulgate an alternative understanding of identity after trauma (Sinason 2002) and to trouble the medicalised version of experience that describes, creates, and sustains difference (Antze and Lambek 1996; Reavey and Warner 2003). The specific contribution made here, though, is the provision of a nuanced and detailed exemplification of Mardorossian's (2014) critique of the contemporary framing of 'rape victim' identity as inevitably vulnerable, inherently deficient, and so stigmatised that immediate transformation is required. It details the challenge she proposes to essentialism that presumes sexual violence is an enduring expression of masculinity and victimisation of women. Also exposed within this example of the subtleties of categorisation is an individualism that assumes 'victim' wrongness rather than fault the morality of the society that encourages such violence. There are of course many and varied feminist responses to victim blaming (Kelly 1997a; Jones and Cook 2008), but the contribution made here is an exposition of secondary harm and an extension to the theorisation of responsibility that includes collusive others.

Evident within accounts from women who have experienced sexual violence is both an acceptance and rejection of the category 'rape victim' as a contemporary and all-consuming subjectivity. The predominance of psychological terminology renders alternative descriptive language and sense-making elusive. The effects of classification offset the need to have rape recognised as a dehumanising process. Either way, personal costs are incurred. Acquiring 'victim' status legitimises the devastation of rape, but it precludes agency and control. The spectral presence of innocence, on which the universal application of credibility assessment depends, not only detracts from the reality of rape but is available exclusively to the very young as it is presumed women lie (Jordan 2004b). Chances of credibility approval are further reduced in the compartmentalising of experience through trivialisation and sensationalisation. Moreover, the 'rape victim' requires monitoring and surveillance of manifested trauma, and her work towards 'normality' (Warner 2003).

Conversely, in not telling, not naming, or trivialising experience, women linger outside of, avoid, and resist victim categorisation. Some agency and control is retained, but she may feel fraudulent or anticipate both exposure and eventual confrontation with the trauma that will supposedly catch up with her. Standing on a metaphorical cliff edge, this implicit contradiction is evidenced in the reluctance to jump into the categorical abyss, where simultaneously endured are the fears of not being believed and of the personal harm caused in keeping this experience contained. The prioritisation of this moment in accounts from women reveals the operation of categorisation which ultimately prevents women from speaking out and accessing recognition and respect. For those who decide to disclose, their experiences, and the articulation of them, are constricted. The challenge that varied and nuanced experiences offer is therefore silenced and erased from the debate.

Troubling the contemporary articulation of the 'rape victim' also necessitates questioning sexual violence as an inevitable expression of an essentially dominant masculinity and naturally victimised femininity. Although it was acknowledged within women's accounts that men and boys experienced the devastation of sexual violence, the primary cause for concern was the denial of female (sexual) agency which was communicated in two main ways. Firstly, women were dissatisfied with

DOI: 10.1057/9781137461728.0007

the political language of sexual violence that prioritised male aggression but inadequately explained their experiences of abuse perpetrated and condoned by women. Accounts here problematised the normalisation of male aggression and the customary explanations of female perpetrated abuse (Peter 2006, 2008) that either trivialise because women are not perceived to have sexual capacity or sensationalise the female perpetrator's unusually monstrous sexuality.

Secondly, in the aftermath of rape, women expressed the need to articulate their sexuality independently from their experiences of sexual violence in order to challenge the subsumption of female sexuality as responsible for male sexual behaviour or as unavoidably traumatic and problematic (Reavey 2003). The denial of female sexual agency limits opportunities to make sense of particular experiences of abuse, but it also clearly demonstrates the significance and predominance of male sexuality as the defining framework. Indeed, the feminist politics of SlutWalk questionably appropriated and disseminated the assertive sexuality of masculinity because it appeared to encompass freedom from gendered restrictions. Accounts therefore suggest the necessity of theorisation of a female sexual agency that, in the same manner as subjectivity, is not essentially derived but emerges within the social and political context.

The framing of contemporary 'rape victim' identity (Mardorossian 2014) insists on psychological descriptions of trauma (O'Dell 2003) that dismiss the significance of the social and political context. Located within neoliberalism, this focus on the individual prioritises victim-blaming rather than social responsibility, especially apparent in situations of sexual violence. It is evident in accounts that women find themselves already deficient, blameworthy, and shameful, and depending on the reactions of others, these feelings are relieved or encouraged. Secondary harm, therefore, is the imposition of cultural expectation and victim-blaming in every subsequent encounter that affirms and reproduces the dehumanisation of sexual violence, and where trauma is interpreted as confirmation of 'victimhood'. Although most encounters involved some element of victim-blaming and trauma assessment, it was mothers' negative responses that were particularly painful.

In accounts women spoke of their mothers not believing them, telling them to keep quiet or risk the break-up of the family, accusing them of provoking the sexual violence, trivialising it, and choosing not to notice. Many women decide not to disclose to their mothers to protect them from what they feel to be the repellent truth. It is also because they fear

DOI: 10.1057/9781137461728.0007

their mothers' rejection, and they may question her allegiance especially when the perpetrator is another family member. The fear that their mothers knew about, condoned, and did nothing to stop childhood sexual abuse is extremely difficult to bear. It is clear in the effect that mothers' responses invoke, that experiencing sexual violence can be devastating, but the secondary harm caused by reactions that trivialise, disbelieve, or blame reproduces the devastation and shame and highlights there may be nowhere to go.

The secondary harm of victim-blaming exists in a symbiotic relationship with the negation of social responsibility that functions to limit options and opportunities to articulate the reality of rape. Alongside examples of victim-blaming, women's accounts emphasised the sociality of sexual violence, not least in the indestructible humanity signified in excruciating and overwhelming shame. Women suggested that their efforts to prevent, evade, and ultimately reduce the harm of sexual violence are culturally redefined as complicity. Perpetrator tactics (Warner 2007), including an entitlement that renders their behaviour incomprehensible even to themselves, immediately confuse and eventually deflect perpetrator responsibility. The role of others is obfuscated explicitly in the participation, observation, and trivialisation of sexual violence and implicitly in our denial, ignorance, and indifference. The readiness with which women are blamed for sexual violence and the reluctance to assign responsibility to the perpetrator-other within the context of Rape Culture indicates clearly the necessity of a multi-level challenge that prioritises our collective and social responsibility. The political critique of most feminism refuses to blame women for sexual violence and problematises the cultural scaffolding of rape (Gavey 2005). Some of the women in this study were not interested in the politics of feminism to make sense of their experiences. However, the values of feminism are encompassed in the following evaluation of the project of writing sexual violence carefully and in the recommendations, precisely because of its challenge to the neoliberal individualism of secondary harm, perpetuated in the predominance of psychological responses.

Limitations

Gay (2014: 133) asserts the importance of writing sexual violence 'carefully' because '[t]he right stories are not being told, or we're not writing

DOI: 10.1057/9781137461728.0007

enough about the topic of rape in the right ways.' The particular problems she identifies are the impossibility and impact of insisting on the distinction between the representation and experience of rape. For example, compartmentalisation tolerates the inaccurate and derogatory depiction of rape, thereby trivialising most experiences, whilst sensationalising the vicarious trauma or re-traumatisation of those encountering stories of sexual violence, which was a concern for participants. The real consequences are dire as this oppositional positioning confirms the privilege of those who have not been raped in the 'othering' of the discredited and 'over-sensitive' 'rape victim'. Composing rape in the right way, then, involves the responsible and sensitive pursuit of the mutuality of representation and reality instead. In choosing not to portray women who experience rape and sexual violence as discredited or stigmatised, and in articulating agency and resistance, her 'othering' in reality might be avoided. However, even writing from experience, the task is onerous and clarified here by Gay (2014: 235):

> As I write any of these stories, I wonder if I am being too gratuitous. I want to *get it right*. But how do you get this sort of thing right? How do you write violence authentically without making it exploitative? I worry that I am contributing to the cultural numbness... that allows rape to be rich fodder for popular culture and entertainment.... Whilst I have these concerns, I also feel committed to telling the truth. These violences happen even if bearing such witness contributes to a spectacle of sexual violence.

The responsibility of writing carefully is evaluated in a return to the concerns of participants. For a study which engages a methodological approach that troubles the representation of rape necessitates a critique of its own representation of rape. Exposed are two main limitations of the research that also highlight issues for practice.

The purpose of this research was to detail nuance absent from cultural representations of rape in order to challenge the categorisation of the 'rape victim'. Therefore, whilst recognising the significance of other forms of sexualised violence, this particular representation engaged with accounts from 12 women who had been raped at any point in their lives. The narratives, indicative of concerns encountered daily as a practitioner, were emotive, eloquent, varied, and rich. Although ethically appropriate, my decision to rely on voluntary participation limited the scale and representation of experiences which indeed tended towards repeated, physically violent, and organised rape. It could be argued, then, that as

DOI: 10.1057/9781137461728.0007

opportunities to present more divergent experiences were restricted, the methodological risks included the possibility of insufficient challenge to the categorisation of 'rape victim', and in the routine presentation of the sensational, compartmentalisation is arguably sustained. For without the range of alternative narratives, violence may feel normalised and trivialised. Mindful of categorisation and compartmentalisation, care was taken with interpretation and analysis to deliberately avoid trivialisation and sensationalisation. In fact, the need to problematise 'rape victim' identity originated and developed within the diverse and detailed narratives. However, the prioritisation of accounts of violence in rape has implications for practice.

Most rape is not physically violent; that it is, therefore, not culturally legitimate as 'real rape' (Estrich 1987) is signified in the normalisation of physically violent experiences. How, then, do we discuss and respond to violence within some experiences of rape without imposing victimisation or contributing to this compartmentalisation? Women's accounts suggest that articulating violence in rape is an expression of an unbearable reality perceived differently as the cultural compartmentalisation of these severe and rare experiences differentiates them from the supposedly usual and less harmful. Although all violence is serious, in its sensationalisation she is confronted with acknowledging his complete domination proved in the physical violence and therefore to also acknowledge her fundamental victimisation which is overwhelmingly disempowering. It also further stigmatises her because she is different from other raped women with whom she has some connection but who may not feel so 'victimised' in comparison. Whether it is too difficult to hear or too 'normal', ignoring violence contributes to the compartmentalisation of rape because it supports the distinction between the tolerable and intolerable and silences those who fear stigmatisation in their exclusion from other women who have experienced sexual violence. Therefore, it is imperative that the significance of violence is acknowledged in our responses, but without sensationalisation and trivialisation. So although the experiences of those who contributed were not necessarily representative, in their articulation of violence, they facilitated a challenge to the compartmentalisation and re-creation of victimisation that affects all women who have experienced rape.

Plugging the gaps caused by categorisation and compartmentalisation in order to present more accurately the reality of rape suggests political

DOI: 10.1057/9781137461728.0007

motivation. Indeed, as a practitioner in the field of sexual violence, I chose to analyse material from a critical feminist perspective not shared with some of the participants. At times my interpretation contradicted participants' own understanding of their experiences, evident within Violet's comments at the beginning of this conclusion, and in contrarily naming Dawn's experience as rape when she was reluctant to do so. It could be argued, therefore, that the research is limited because it does not engage with theory outside of feminism, and who am I anyway to speak on others' behalf? I have suggested that sexual violence impacts the individual and effectively reproduces structural inequalities. Feminism routinely tackles issues of violence against women, offers the possibility of personal and social transformation, and supports an ethical methodology involving participants in a process of mutual interpretation and approval of priorities.

However, in practical terms, no matter who is speaking about rape or how ethical and careful the representation might be, are we contributing to the 'cultural numbness' that denies the reality of rape as Gay fears? Of concern is not only the pervasive trivialisation of rape or the apparent avoidance of perpetrator responsibility, but, in a poignant example, Brison (2002) articulates the significance to other women of contributing to the cultural representation of rape. It was during the event of rape, when Brison (2002) recalled other women's stories of their experiences, that she came to understand the enormity of what was happening to her. In the aftermath, writing her own account, she was acutely aware of the endowment her representation would make to women's future sexual scripts and meaning-making processes. Clearly representation and reality are not mutually exclusive, but emotively intertwined and problematically wrestled. Nevertheless, for Gay (2014), Brison (2002), and in women's accounts here, it is imperative that experiences of rape are rendered intelligible, as a testament to an undeniable social reality. Careful representation of rape therefore offers an alternative to rape mythology and counteracts ignorance; otherwise, secrets are kept and women are isolated, blamed, and shamed. Eliza wanted her experiences retold to help other women and to enhance the responses of practitioners, an outcome which was also important to Amy. Therefore, my role in this research was as a conduit, taking note of discrepancies, to disseminate representations of rape that provided a different perspective in order to reduce shame and improve practice responses.

DOI: 10.1057/9781137461728.0007

Recommendations for practice

Women's accounts clearly communicate the impact of categorisation and compartmentalisation on their lives in the aftermath of rape. Presented here are recommendations for action to prevent secondary harm that occurs in personal and societal responses to sexual violence. In rape, women already feel ashamed, disempowered, and responsible; therefore, how we respond is crucial. We can choose to silence her with devastating consequences or offer her understanding and solidarity.

Therefore, in order not to silence or hinder her articulation of rape, in our personal response, we should:

1 Listen to what she says without judgement, presumption, or interruption to identify what she feels and needs. We should also be patient and calm, using gentle questioning only to clarify we have understood accurately. Remembering and then articulating intimate details is difficult, especially as the sexual language available to women is limited.

2 Make no assessment of severity, but acknowledge the particular difficulties she identifies. Trivialising it as 'a bit of fumbling' or 'it can't have been that bad or you would have said something at the time' dismisses her experiences, and ignores the barriers to disclosure. Sensationalising her experiences through shock, disgust, or particular interest stigmatises her.

3 Make no assessment of credibility. Nothing about her behaviour or character prompted the rape.

4 Make no assessment of trauma. We should neither expect nor deny presentation of trauma. Absence of trauma is no indication of deceit. Presence of trauma does not signify mental ill-health. If it becomes apparent she has, for example, intrusive memories, acknowledge them as a common response.

5 Not impose or police the boundaries of victimhood by dictating the remit of the conversation or confining her articulation of rape to particular environments or to specific 'experts'. Not only does this denigrate her as contaminated, but others are inhibiting her opportunities for self-determination.

6 Believe her disclosure automatically and demonstrably. She has overcome numerous obstacles and self-doubt to reach this situation.

DOI: 10.1057/9781137461728.0007

7   Avoid using categories such as 'victim' or 'survivor'. Labelling restricts her self-presentation and determines our response. But if she uses them, attempt to understand what these labels mean to her.

8   Be mindful of the rape myths and gendered, racist, homophobic, and classist stereotypes we hold and strive to educate ourselves. It is not acceptable to impose our ignorance onto others reaching out for support, reassurance, or friendship.

9   Recognise the strategies of resistance she has developed and used, rather than focus only on the harm. We are all the sum of a lifetime accumulation of experience and deserve respect. Who we are cannot be reduced to particular events or incidents.

10 Take seriously and act upon the decisions she makes about her experiences. Women are often let down by people and/or agencies that do not follow up on agreed action, are complacent, or ignore her. This is frustrating and communicates to her that she is worthless. It can also leave women unsafe.

11 Consider the impact of, and avoid re-creating, shame. We should be comfortable talking about sex, bodies, and sexuality to reduce the shame in relating intimate details of rape. We should strive to understand her explanations of the role she feels she had in sexual violence and reassure her that she did nothing to provoke the situation, nor was she complicit. It is the behaviour of the perpetrator that is shameful.

12 Recognise her need to define her own relationship to her body and sexuality, being careful not impose the predominant, male sexual framework upon her.

13 Recognise female perpetrated abuse without trivialisation or sensationalisation. We should take seriously women's capacity to abuse, condone, and ignore sexual violence and the different emotions this evokes. Politically sexual violence perpetrated by men or women should be equally condemnable.

14 Be aware that debates about vicarious trauma feeds sensationalisation to prevent women from speaking out and to trivialise the reality of living with the effects of rape. It is also positions women who experience trauma as exceptionally sensitive and vulnerable, which reproduces victimisation.

DOI: 10.1057/9781137461728.0007

In response to the harmful effects of the social reproduction of categorisation and compartmentalisation in sexual violence as they have been
specifically identified in this research, we should:

15 Review policy that relies on the cycle of abuse theory and implicitly
   locates responsibility with women. In practice it prioritises
   evidentially 'serious' events and promotes a criminal justice
   response, leaving little support for the majority of women who do
   not want to report to the police.
16 Highlight the clear discrepancy between what rapists say about
   their behaviour and what they actually did in order to challenge
   the notion that rape results from mixed messages which displaces
   responsibility away from the perpetrator.
17 Always locate responsibility for sexual violence with the
   perpetrator. Those who have the capacity to choose to be actively
   involved in abuse as organisers or recruiters, or who profit from
   sexual violence, are equally responsible. Those who have the
   capacity to choose to observe, endorse, and condone are complicit.
18 Return to a political response based on feminist principles of
   self-determination and empowerment. Bureaucratic risk-focussed
   procedures reinforce victim-blaming and exclude from support
   women who require longer-term involvement that is outside of the
   criminal justice and mental health care systems.

Why it was important to carry out this research

At the time of writing, underway are the drawn out and faltering
preliminaries of the UK public inquiry into the institutional failure to
protect children from sexual abuse, headed by the Honourable Lowell
Goddard. Already apparent are the processes of compartmentalisation
and categorisation. Whilst the media sensationally predict the investigation will shake the foundations of democracy, and focus on the
systematic cover-up by senior governmental officials of the sexual abuse
and murder of young boys in state care institutions, those who have
experienced sexual violence are excluded from the process because they
lack objectivity. In this nationwide investigation involving many, already
diminished are individuals' voices, with women's experiences further
trivialised in their 'normality'. But the generalised perception that 'they'

DOI: 10.1057/9781137461728.0007

as a homogenous group of 'survivors' are different in their incapacity for objectivity fundamentally reproduces the categorisation of the 'rape victim' as deficient and stigmatised. This insistence on objectivity is supposed to legitimate the investigation whose message suggests a critical, scientific, and rigorous procedure. Side-lining practice that believes children's disclosures, prioritised instead is the systematic presumption of deceit. In this morass of corruption, senior officials and 'survivors' alike will be scrutinised in the search for truth. Disguised as professionalism, objectivity has excluded and silenced those who have experienced sexual violence, and feminist practitioners, who employ an alternative and respectful approach, are presumed misguided, gullible, and lacking in due diligence.

The cost of disclosure is evident, for excluded are the individuals who have made their experiences known. In this appalling example of categorisation, women who publicly name their experiences are ludicrously differentiated from professionals, require representatives, and are ultimately contained. Women who have undisclosed experiences of sexual violence may feel compromised or at risk of exposure. In this context women are silenced, whether or not they have disclosed. Of course there are critical voices. Developing an ethical response requires a commitment to challenging these attitudes and practices that restrict women's lives, whoever we are. We can start with recognising our social responsibility and take action in our personal responses to avoid secondary harm. Lyra reminds us of the imperative to articulate the personal and social reality that is sexual violence:

> I have this thing burning inside me telling me to keep talking. And I can remember being in hospital when I was fourteen and going to these meetings where he rolled in and did the whole 'concerned father' act and lots of adults nodding, and the weight and the darkness of it being there like you could cut it with a knife, and suffocating and choking on my own silence. And I think I can't ever be in that position again. Anything would be better. And then I think of that and I think that the fear of talking is from a whole range of collusive 'others' – professionals who talk the talk really well, institutions, people in my everyday life – making me afraid because they want to forget and don't want to confront that I'm just as human as they are but what happened in my life still happened. And then I think fuck that. And then I talk in meetings and stuff and people's faces do funny things and I think 'oh god it's happening' again. And I do feel scared but often I laugh a little bit inside too because I'm not silent.

DOI: 10.1057/9781137461728.0007

Bibliography

Ahmed, S. (2004) *The Cultural Politics of Emotion.* Edinburgh University Press.

Allen, L. (2003) 'Girls Want Sex, Boys Want Love: Resisting Dominant Discourses of (Hetero) Sexuality' in *Sexualities* 6: 215–33, London; Thousand Oaks, CA; and New Delhi: Sage.

Amara, P. (2015) ' "I Want My Body Back": Survivors' Stories of Sex after Rape' in *New Statesmen* 5 March http://www.newstatesman.com/voices/2014/03/i-want-my-body-back-survivors-stories-sex-after-rape [Accessed 5 March 2015].

Anderson, I. and Doherty, K. (2008) *Accounting for Rape: Psychology, Feminism and Discourse Analysis in the Study of Sexual Violence.* East Sussex: Routledge.

Antze, P. and Lambek, M. (1996) *Tense Past: Cultural Essays in Trauma and Memory.* New York: Routledge.

Attwood, F. (2007) 'Sluts and Riot Grrls: Female Identity and Sexual Agency' in *Journal of Gender Studies* 16(3): 231–47, Routledge.

Bartky, S. L. (1990) *Femininity and Domination: Studies in the Phenomenology of Oppression.* London: Routledge.

Batmanghelidjh, C. (2006) *Shattered Lives: Children Who Live With Courage and Dignity.* London: Jessica Kingsley Publishers.

Becker, D. (2005) *The Myth of Empowerment: Women and the Therapeutic Culture in America.* New York University Press.

Bindel, J. (2015) 'So a judge said a 16 year-old groomed her teacher – that's nothing' *The Guardian* 15 January http://www.theguardian.com/commentisfree/2015/jan/15/judge-16-year-old-groomed-teacher-judges-lawyers [Accessed January 15th 2015].

Bolen, R. M. (2003) 'Non Offending Mothers of Sexually Abused Children: A Case of Institutionalised Sexism' in *Violence Against Women* 9(11): 1336-66, Sage.

Bourke, J. (2010) *Rape: A History from 1860 to the Present*. London: Virago.

Brison, S. J. (2002) *Aftermath: Violence and the Remaking of a Self*. Princeton, NJ: Princeton University Press.

Brownmiller, S. (1975) *Against Our Will: Men, Women and Rape*. New York: Simon and Schuster.

Budgeon, S. (2011) 'The Contradictions of Successful Femininity: Third Wave Feminism, Postfeminism and "New" Femininities' in R. Gill and C. Scharff (Eds) *New Femininities: Postfeminism, Neoliberalism and Subjectivity*. Hampshire: Palgrave Macmillan.

Burman, E. (2003) 'Childhood, Sexual Abuse and Contemporary Political Subjectivities' in P. Reavey and S. Warner (Eds) *New Feminist Stories of Child Sexual Abuse: Sexual Scripts and Dangerous Dialogues*. London: Routledge.

Butler, J. (1997) *Excitable Speech: Politics of the Performance*. London: Routledge.

Butler, J. (2004) *Undoing Gender Routlege*. New York.

Butler, J. (2006) *Precarious Life: The Powers of Mourning and Violence*. London: Verso.

Cahill, A. J. (2001) *Rethinking Rape*. New York: Cornell University Press.

Campbell, R., Adams, A. E., Wasco, S. M., Ahrens, C. E., and Sefi, T. (2009) 'Training Interviews for Research on Sexual Violence: A Qualitative Study of Rape Survivors' Recommendations for Interview Practice' in *Violence Against Women* 15(5): 595–617, Sage Publications.

Campbell, R., Adams, A. E., Wasco, S. M., Ahrens, C. E., and Sefi, T. (2010) ' "What Has It Been Like for You to Talk with Me Today?" The Impact of Participating in Interview Research on Rape Survivors' " in *Violence Against Women* 16(1): 60–83, Sage Publications.

Campbell, S. (2010) 'Memory, Truth and the Search for an Authentic Past' in J. Haaken and P. Reavey (Eds) *Memory Matters: Contexts for Understanding Sexual Abuse Recollections* East Sussex: Routledge.

Clark, A. (1987) *Women's Silence, Men's Violence: Sexual Assault in England 1770-1845*. London: Pandora Press.

DOI: 10.1057/9781137461728.0008

Coffey, A. (1999) *The Ethnographic Self: Fieldwork and the Representation of Identity*. London: Sage Publications.

Coffey, A. (2014) *Real Voices: Child Sexual Exploitation in Greater Manchester. An Independent Report* http://anncoffeymp.com/wp-content/uploads/2014/10/Real-Voices-Final.pdf [Accessed 1 November 2014].

Coy, M. Kelly, L., and Foord, Jo., with Balding, V. and Davenport, R. (2007) *Maps of Gaps: The Postcode Lottery of Violence against Women Support Services*. London: End Violence Against Women in partnership with Equality and Human Rights Commission.

Coy, M. (2009) 'Invaded Spaces and Feeling Dirty: Women's Narratives of Violation in Prostitution and Sexual Violence' in M. Horvath and J. Brown (Eds) *Rape: Challenging Contemporary Thinking* Devon: Willan Publishing.

Croghan, R. and Miell, D. (1995) 'Blaming Our Mothers, Blaming Ourselves: Women's Accounts of Childhood Abuse and Disruption' in *Feminism and Psychology* 5(1): 31–46, Sage.

Denov, M. S. (2004) *Perspectives on Female Sex Offending: A Culture of Denial*. Hampshire: Ashgate Publishing.

Dines, G. and Murphy, W. J. (2011) 'SlutWalk Is Not Sexual Liberation' in *The Guardian* 8 May http://www.theguardian.com/commentisfree/2011/may/08/slutwalk-not-sexual-liberation [Accessed 10 June 2011].

Doyle, C. (2006) *Working with Abused Children* (3rd edition) Hampshire: Palgrave Macmillan.

Estrich, S. (1987) *Real Rape: How the Legal System Victimises Women Who Say No*. Cambridge, MA: Harvard University Press.

Filar, R. (2011) 'SlutWalking Is Rooted in Riot Grrl Attitude' in *T he Guardian* 9 May http://www.theguardian.com/commentisfree/2011/may/09/slutwalk-feminist-activism [Accessed 10 June 2011].

Fine, M., and Weis, L. (2010) 'Writing the "Wrongs" of Fieldwork: Confronting Our Own Research Writing Dilemmas in Urban Ethnography' in W. Luttrell (Ed.) *Qualitative Educational Research: Readings in Reflexive Methodology and Transformative Practice*. New York and Abingdon: Routledge.

Finley, N. J. (2010) 'Skating Femininity: Gender Manoeuvring in Women's Roller Derby' in *Journal of Contemporary Ethnography* 39: 359–87, Sage.

DOI: 10.1057/9781137461728.0008

Fitzroy, L. (2001) 'Violent Women: Questions for Feminist Theory, Practice and Policy' in *Critical Social Policy* 21(1): 7–34, Sage.

Foucault, M. (1991) *Discipline and Punish: The Birth of the Prison*. London: Penguin.

Foucault, M. (1997) 'On the Genealogy of Ethics' in P. Rabinow (Ed) *Ethics: Subjectivity and Truth – The Essential Works of Foucault 1954–1984, Volume One*. London: Penguin.

Foucault, M. (2007) 'Subjectivity and Truth' in S. Lotringer (Ed.) *The Politics of Truth*. Los Angeles: Semiotext(e).

Frith, H. (2009) 'Sexual Scripts: Sexual Refusals and Rape' in M. Horvath and J. Brown (Eds) *Rape: Challenging Contemporary Thinking*. Devon: Willan Publishing.

Furedi, F. (2004) *Therapy Culture: Cultivating Vulnerability in an Uncertain Age*. London: Routledge.

Gavey, N. (1999) ' "I Wasn't Raped, But ..." Revisiting Definitional Problems in Sexual Victimisation' in S. Lamb (Ed) *New Versions of Victims: Feminist Struggle with the Concept*. New York University Press.

Gavey, N. (2005) *Just Sex? The Cultural Scaffolding of Rape*. East Sussex: Routledge.

Gavey, N. and Schmidt, J. (2011) ' "Trauma of Rape" Discourse: A Double-Edged Template for Everyday Understanding of the Impact of Rape?' in *Violence Against Women* 17(4): 433–56, Sage.

Gay, R. (2014) 'The Careless Language of Sexual Violence' in *Bad Feminist*. New York: Corsair.

Goffman, E. (1963) *Stigma: Notes on the Management of Spoiled Identity*. Harmondsworth: Penguin.

Gold, T. (2011) 'Marching with the SlutWalkers' in *The Guardian* Tuesday 7 June http://www.theguardian.com/world/2011/jun/07/marching-with-the-slutwalkers [Accessed 10 June 2011].

Grattagliano, I., Owens, J. N., Morton, R. J., Campobasso, C. P., Carabellese, F., and Catanesi, R. (2012) 'Female Sexual Offenders: Five Italian Case Studies' in *Aggression and Violent Behaviour* 17(3): 180–87, Sage.

Grayston, A. D. and De Luca, R. V. (1999) 'Female Perpetrators of Child Sexual Abuse: A Review of the Clinical and Empirical Literature' in *Aggression and Violent Behaviour* 4: 93–106, Sage.

Greer, G. (2011) 'These SlutWalk Women Are Simply Fighting for the Right to Be Dirty' in *The Telegraph* 12 May http://www.telegraph.co.uk/women/womens-health/8510743/These-slut-walk-women-are-simply-fighting-for-their-right-to-be-dirty.html [Accessed 10 June 2011].

Guenther, L. (2012) 'Resisting Agamben: The Biopolitics of Shame and Humiliation' in *Philosophy and Social Criticism* 38(1): 59–79, Sage.

Haaken, J. (1998) *Pillar of Salt: Gender, Memory and the Perils of Looking Back.* London: Free Associated Books Ltd.

Healicon, A. (2012) *Resistance and Identity in a Voluntary Sector Sexual Violence Support Service.* Unpublished PhD thesis, Manchester Metropolitan University.

Herman, J. L. (2001) *Trauma and Recovery: From Domestic Abuse to Political Terror.* London: Pandora.

Islam, A. (2011) 'Why I'll Be Joining the London SlutWalk' in *The Guardian* Saturday 11 June http://www.theguardian.com/commentisfree/2011/jun/11/london-slutwalk [Accessed 12 June 2011].

Itzin, C. (2006) *Tackling the Health and Mental Health Effects of Domestic and Sexual Violence and Abuse.* Department of Health Publications Online, London http://www.wdvf.org.uk/HealthEffects.pdf [Accessed 1 October 2010].

Jackson, S. and Vares, T. (2011) 'Media Sluts: Tween Girls' Negotiations of Postfeminist Sexual Subjectivities in Popular Culture' in R. Gill and C. Scharff (Eds) *New Femininities: Postfeminism, Neoliberalism and Subjectivity* Hampshire: Palgrave Macmillan.

James, S. (2011) 'My Placard Read "Pensioner Slut" and I Was Proud of It' in *The Guardian* Sunday 19 June http://www.theguardian.com/commentisfree/2011/jun/19/slutwalk-new-womens-movement [Accessed 13 July 2011].

Jones, H. and Cook, K. (2008) *Rape Crisis: Responding to Sexual Violence.* Lyme Regis, UK: Russell House.

Jones, S. (2011) 'Feminist Critics of SlutWalk Have Forgotten That Language Is Not a Commodity' in *The F Word: Contemporary UK Feminism* 8 June http://www.thefword.org.uk/features/2011/06/the_politics_of_slutwalk [Accessed 13 July 2011].

Jordan, J. (2004a) 'Beyond Belief? Police, Rape and Women's Credibility' in *Criminal Justice* 4(1): 29–59, Sage.

Jordan, J. (2004b) *The Word of a Woman?: Police, Rape and Belief.* Houndmills, UK: Palgrave Macmillan.

Jordan, J. (2008) *Serial Survivors: Women's Narratives of Surviving Rape.* Sydney: Federation Press.

DOI: 10.1057/9781137461728.0008

Kaufman, K. L., Wallace, A. M., Felzen-Johnson, C., and Lesley-Reeder, M. (1995) 'Comparing Female and Male Perpetrators' Modus Operandi: Victims' Reports of Sexual Abuse' in *Journal of Interpersonal Violence* 10(3): 322–33, Sage.

Kelly, L. (1988) *Surviving Sexual Violence.* Cambridge: Polity Press.

Kelly, L. (1997a) 'A Critical Issue: Sexual Violence and Feminist Theory' in S. Kemp and J. Squires (Eds) *Feminisms.* Oxford: Oxford University Press.

Kelly, L. (1997b) 'When Does the Speaking Profit Us? Reflections on the Challenges of Developing Feminist Perspectives on Abuse and Violence by Women' in M. Hester, L. Kelly, and J. Radford (Eds) *Women, Violence and Male Power.* Buckingham: Open University Press.

Kelly, L., Lovett, J., and Regan, L. (2005) *A Gap or a Chasm? Attrition in Reported Rape Cases.* Home Office Research Study 293. London: Development and Statistics Directorate.

Kelly, L. and Radford, J. (1997) 'Nothing Really Happened: The Invalidation of Women's Experiences of Sexual Violence' in M. Hester, L. Kelly, and J. Radford (Eds) *Women, Violence and Male Power* Buckingham: Open University Press.

Kelly, L., and Radford, J. (1998) 'Sexual Violence against Women and Girls: An Approach to an International Overview' in R. E. Dobash and R. P. Dobash (Eds) *Rethinking Violence Against Women.* Thousand Oaks, CA: Sage Publications.

Kemmis, S. and McTaggart, R. (2000) 'Participatory Action Research' in N. Denzin and Y. Lincoln (Eds) *The International Handbook on Qualitative Research.* Thousand Oaks, CA: Sage Publications.

Kruper, M. (2013) 'Top 7 Craziest Comments Made about SlutWalk' in *The Humanist Network News* Monday 12 August http://americanhumanist.org/HNN/details/2013-08-top-7-craziest-comments-made-about-slutwalk [Accessed 12 November 2014].

Lamb, S. (1999) 'Constructing the Victim: Popular Images and Lasting Labels' in S. Lamb (Ed.) *New Versions of Victims: Feminist Struggle with the Concept.* New York University Press.

Laville, S. (2014) 'Call for Prosecutors to Answer for Trial of Alleged Rape Victim Who Killed Herself' *The Guardian* 6 November http://www.theguardian.com/law/2014/nov/06/call-crown-prosecutors-account-suicide-alleged-rape-victim [Accessed 12 November 2014].

Lees, S. (1993) *Sugar and Spice: Sexuality and Adolescent Girls.* London: Penguin.

DOI: 10.1057/9781137461728.0008

Lockwood Harris, K. (2011) 'The Next Problem with No Name: The Politics and Pragmatics of the Word Rape' in *Women's Studies in Communication* 34(1): 42–63, Elsevier.

Lyra. (2014) How to Survive without Being a Survivor [Online] 7 December. Available from: wordpress.com https://whatsthefirstrule. wordpress.com/author/lyrafightclub/ [Accessed 13 January 2015].

MacKinnon, C. A. (1989) *Toward a Feminist Theory of the State.* Cambridge, MA: Harvard University Press.

MacKinnon, C. A. (1995) 'Sex and Violence: A Perspective' in P. Searles and R. J. Berger (Eds) *Rape and Society: Readings on the Problem of Sexual Assault.* Boulder, CO: Westview Press.

Mardorossian, C. M. (2014) *Framing the Rape Victim: Gender and Agency Reconsidered.* New Brunswick, NJ: Rutgers University Press.

Marhia, N. (2008) *Just Representation: Press Reporting and the Reality of Rape* Eaves. London: Matrix Chambers.

Mathews, R., Matthews, J. K., and Speltz, K. (1989) *Female Sexual Offenders: An Exploratory Study.* Orwell, VT: Safer Society Press.

Matthews, N. A. (1994) *Confronting Rape: The Feminist Anti-Rape Movement and the State.* New York: Routledge.

May, T. and Featherstone, L. (2011) *The Government Response to the Stern Review: An Independent Review into How Rape Complaints Are Handled by Public Authorities in England and Wales.* London: Cabinet Office http://www.homeoffice.gov.uk/publications/crime/call-end-violence-women-girls/government-stern-review?view=Binary [Accessed 6 November 2011].

McRobbie, A. (2009) *The Aftermath of Feminism: Gender, Culture and Social Change.* London: Sage.

McVeigh, T. (2011) 'SlutWalk: Bad Message or a Great Idea?' in *The Guardian* 15 May http://www.theguardian.com/society/2011/may/15/slutwalk-debate-sexual-discrimination [Accessed 10 June 2011].

Murphy, M. (2012) 'It's Not Slut-Shaming, It's Woman-Hating' in *Feminist Current,* 7 December http://feministcurrent.com/6845/its-not-slut-shaming-its-woman-hating/ [Accessed 26 January 2015].

Myhill, A. and Allen, J. (2002) *Rape and Sexual Assault of Women: The Extent and Nature of the Problem.* Home Office Research Study 237. London: Home Office Research, Development and Statistics Directorate.

National Archives (2003) *Sexual Offences Act.* Surrey http://www.legislation.gov.uk/ukpga/2003/42/contents [Accessed 26 January 2015].

DOI: 10.1057/9781137461728.0008

O'Dell, L. (2003) 'The "Harm" Story in Childhood Sexual Abuse: Contested Understandings, Disputed Knowledges' in P. Reavey and S. Warner (Eds) *New Feminist Stories of Child Sexual Abuse: Sexual Scripts and Dangerous Dialogues.* London: Routledge.

Pedwell, C. (2011) 'The Limits of Cross-Cultural Analogy: Muslim Veiling and "Western" Fashion Practices' in R. Gill and C. Scharff (Eds) *New Femininities: Postfeminism, Neoliberalism and Subjectivity.* Hampshire: Palgrave Macmillan.

Peter, T. (2006) 'Mad, Bad or Victim? Making Sense of Mother-Daughter Sexual Abuse' in *Feminist Criminology* 1(4): 283–302, Sage.

Peter, T. (2008) 'Speaking about the Unspeakable: Exploring the Impact of Mother-Daughter Sexual Abuse' in *Violence Against Women* 14(9): 1033–53, Sage.

Phipps, A. (2010) 'Violent and Victimised Bodies: Sexual Violence Policy in England and Wales' in *Critical Social Policy* 30(3): 358–83, Sage.

Phipps, A. (2015) *Genders, Bodies, Politics.* wordpress.com https://genderate.wordpress.com/2015/02/19/neoliberalism-and-the-commodification-of-experience/ [Accessed 16 January 2015].

Plummer, C. A. and Eastin, J. (2007) 'The Effect of Child Sexual Abuse Allegations/Investigations on the Mother/Child Relationship' in *Violence Against Women* 13(10): 1053–71, Sage.

Popadopoulos, L. (2010) *Sexualisation of Young People Review.* London: Home Office.

Probyn, E. (2000a) 'Shaming Theory, Thinking Disconnections: Feminism and Reconciliation' in S. Ahmed, J. Kilby, C. Lury, M. McNeil, and B. Skeggs (Eds) *Transformations: Thinking through Feminism.* New York: Routledge.

Probyn, E. (2000b) *Carnal Appetites: FoodSexIdentities.* London: Routledge.

Proctor, G. (2007) 'Disordered Boundaries? A Critique of Borderline Personality Disorder' in H. Spandler and S. Warner (Eds) *Beyond Fear and Control: Working with Young People Who Self Harm.* Herefordshire: PCCS Books Ltd.

Reavey, P. (2003) 'When Past Meets Present to Produce a Sexual "Other": Examining Professional and Everyday Narratives of Child Sexual Abuse and Sexuality' in in P. Reavey and S. Warner (Eds) *New Feminist Stories of Child Sexual Abuse: Sexual Scripts and Dangerous Dialogues.* London: Routledge.

DOI: 10.1057/9781137461728.0008

Reavey, P. and Gough, B. (2000) 'Dis/Locating Blame: Survivors Constructions of Self and Sexual Abuse' in *Sexualities* 3(3): 325–46, Sage.

Reavey, P. and Warner, S. (Eds) (2003) *New Feminist Stories of Child Sexual Abuse: Sexual Scripts and Dangerous Dialogues*. London: Routledge.

Rich, A. (1980) 'Compulsory Heterosexuality and Lesbian Existence' *Signs* 5(4): 631–60, University of Chicago Press.

Ringrose, J. (2011) 'Are You Sexy, Flirty, or a Slut? Exploring "Sexualisation" and How Teen Girls Perform/Negotiate Digital Sexual Identity on Social Networking Sites' in R. Gill and C. Scharff (Eds) *New Femininities: Postfeminism, Neoliberalism and Subjectivity.* Hampshire: Palgrave Macmillan.

Roiphe, K. (1993) 'Date Rape's Other Victim' in *The New York Times* 13 June http://www.nytimes.com/1993/06/13/magazine/date-rape-s-other-victim.html?pagewanted=5 [Accessed 26 January 2015].

Rothschild, B. (2000) *The Body Remembers: The Psychophysiology of Trauma and Trauma Treatment.* New York and London: Norton.

Rowntree, M. (2009) ' "Living Life with Grace is my Revenge": Situating Survivor Knowledge about Sexual Violence' in *Qualitative Social Work* 8(4): 1–14, Sage.

Sartre, J. P. (2003) *Being and Nothingness.* London and New York: Routledge.

Scott, S. (2001) *The Politics and Experiences of Ritual Abuse: Beyond Disbelief.* Buckingham: Open University Press.

Scully, D. and Morolla, J. (1995) ' "Riding the Bull at Gilley's": Convicted Rapists Describe the Rewards of Rape' in P. Searles and R. J. Berger (Eds) *Rape and Society: Readings on the Problem of Sexual Assault.* Boulder, CO: Westview Press.

Shacklock. G. and Smyth, J. (1998) *Being Reflexive in Critical Educational and Social Research.* London: Falmer Press.

Siegel D. J. (1999) *The Developing Mind.* New York: Guilford Press.

Sinason, V. (Ed.) (2002) *Attachment, Trauma and Multiplicity: Working with Dissociative Identity Disorder.* East Sussex: Routledge.

Skinner, T., Hester, M., and Malos, E. (2005) *Researching Gender Violence: Feminist Methodology in Action.* Collumpton: Willan Publishing.

Smith, L. (2015) 'Barrister Sparks Outcry by Claiming Men Should Be Cleared of Rape if the Victim Was Drunk' *The Independent* 6 February http://www.independent.co.uk/news/uk/crime/barrister-sparks-outcry-by-claiming-men-should-be-cleared-of-rape-if-the-victim-was-drunk-10030529.html [Accessed 6 February 2015].

DOI: 10.1057/9781137461728.0008

Taylor-Johnson, J. (1992) *Mothers of Incest Survivors: Another Side of the Story.* Bloomington: Indiana University Press.

Valenti, J. (2011) 'SlutWalks and the Future of Feminism' in *The Washington Post* 3 June http://www.washingtonpost.com/opinions/slutwalks-and-the-future-of-feminism/2011/06/01/AGjB9LIH_story.html [Accessed 10 June 2011].

Van Dijk, J. (2009) 'Free the Victim: A Critique of the Western Conception of Victimhood' in *International Review of Victimology* 16: 1–33, Sage.

Vandiver, D. M. and Kercher, G. (2004) 'Offender and Victim Characteristics of Registered Female Sexual Offenders in Texas: A Proposed Typology of Female Sexual Offenders' in *Sexual Abuse: A Journal of Research and Treatment* 16(2): 121–37, Sage.

Walia, H. (2011) 'Slutwalk: To March or Not to March' *Rabble.CA* 18 May http://rabble.ca/news/2011/05/slutwalk-march-or-not-march [Accessed 28 September 2011].

Warner, S. (2003) 'Disrupting Identity through Visible Therapy: A Feminist Post Structuralist Approach to Working with Women Who Have Experienced Child Sexual Abuse' in P. Reavey and S. Warner (Eds) *New Feminist Stories of Child Sexual Abuse: Sexual Scripts and Dangerous Dialogues* London: Routledge.

Warner, S. (2007) *Understanding Child Sexual Abuse: Making the Tactics Visible.* Manchester: Sam Warner Press.

Warner, S. and Wilkins, T. (2003) 'Diagnosing Distress and Reproducing Disorder: Women, Child Sexual Abuse and "Borderline Personality Disorder"' in P. Reavey and S. Warner (Eds) *New Feminist Stories of Child Sexual Abuse: Sexual Scripts and Dangerous Dialogues.* London: Routledge.

Whittier, N. (2009) *The Politics of Child Sexual Abuse: Emotion, Social Movements and the State.* Oxford and New York: Oxford University Press.

Winkler, C. (2002) *One Night: Realities of Rape.* Walnut Creek, CA: Altamira Press.

Women's Resource Centre and Rape Crisis England and Wales (2008) *The Crisis in Rape Crisis.* London: Women's Resource Centre.

Woodhouse, L. (2011) 'SlutWalk London' in *The F Word: Contemporary UK Feminism* 30 April http://www.thefword.org.uk/blog/2011/04/slutwalk_london [Accessed 12 July 2011].

Woodiwiss, J. (2009) *Contesting Stories of Childhood Sexual Abuse.* Basingstoke: Palgrave Macmillan.

DOI: 10.1057/9781137461728.0008

Woodiwiss, J. (2014) 'Beyond a Single Story: The Importance of Separating "Harm" from "Wrongfulness" and "Sexual Innocence" from "Childhood" in Contemporary Narratives of Childhood Sexual Abuse' *Sexualities* 17(1–2): 139–58.

Woodward, C. (2000) 'Hearing Voices? Research Issues When Telling Respondents' Stories of Child Sexual Abuse from a Feminist Perspective' in C. Truman, D. M. Mertens, and B. Humphries (Eds) *Research and Inequality*. London: University College London Press.

Worrell. M (2003) 'Working at Being Survivors: Identity, Gender and Participation' in P. Reavey and S. Warner (Eds) *New Feminist Stories of Child Sexual Abuse: Sexual Scripts and Dangerous Dialogues*. London: Routledge.

Zizek, S. (2009) *Violence: Six Sideways Reflections*. London: Profile Books.

DOI: 10.1057/9781137461728.0008

Index

DOI: 10.1057/9781137461728.0009

DOI: 10.1057/9781137461728.0009

Lightning Source UK Ltd.
Milton Keynes UK
UKOW02n0624220416

272759UK00010B/213/P